MW00987397

"I have been a fan of Ace Collins's literary talent and creativity for many years. This book is so captivating, and Ace is brilliant to have thought of putting together all of these extraordinary stories about the creation of these classic, beloved songs."

Barbara Mandrell

"Great songs endure the years because they are *great* songs, and behind every one there exists a story. In this book my friend and author hero Ace Collins presents the stories behind these uplifting hymns and spirituals. From 'Swing Low, Sweet Chariot' to 'Beyond the Sunset,' Ace delivers in a writing style and manner that are both informative and a blessing to the reader."

Joe Bonsall, forty-six-year member of the Oak Ridge Boys and author of ten books

"Ace Collins has tackled many subjects through the decades as part of his amazing writing career. Now, he has really hit a home run with *Stories behind the Songs and Hymns about Heaven*. For those of us who grew up with these hymns, this book is especially enlightening and inspiring. Reading it makes me wish I were in a wooden church pew right now, singing as best I can."

Rex Nelson, senior editor, *Arkansas Democrat-Gazette*

STORIES
BEHIND
THE
SONGS
& HYMNS
ABOUT
HEAVEN

ACE COLLINS

BakerBooks

a division of Baker Publishing Group
Grand Rapids, Michigan

Published by Baker Books
a division of Baker Publishing Group
PO Box 6287, Grand Rapids, MI 49516-6287
www.bakerbooks.com

Printed in the United States of America

Library of Congress Cataloging-in-Publication Data
Names: Collins, Ace, author.
Title: Stories behind the songs and hymns about heaven / Ace Collins.
Description: Grand Rapids : Baker Books, a division of Baker Publishing
    Group, 2019. | Includes bibliographical references.
Identifiers: LCCN 2019020649 | ISBN 9780801094675 (cloth)
Subjects: LCSH: Hymns—History and criticism. | Songs—History and
    criticism. | Heaven—Songs and music.
Classification: LCC BV310 .C65 2019 | DDC 264/.23—dc23
LC record available at https://lccn.loc.gov/2019020649

Scripture quotations are from the COMMON ENGLISH
BIBLE. © Copyright 2011 COMMON ENGLISH BIBLE.
All rights reserved. Used by permission. (www.Common
EnglishBible.com).

Author is represented by WordServe Literary Group. (www
.wordserveliterary.com)

19 20 21 22 23 24 25   7 6 5 4 3 2 1

This book was inspired by and is dedicated to Ruth Ann "Ruthie" Arnold, a woman of great faith and with a longing for heaven. She passed from this life to the next in 2018 at age eighty-two, hearing many of these songs sung by her husband, George, and her family.

Contents

Introduction

*O*ne of the most fascinating things I found when researching the stories behind songs about heaven is that most were inspired during difficult and trying times. These beloved hymns were often the product of suffering and penned by people looking for answers. Whether a slave, a person trapped in poverty, a preacher, or a teacher, the writer almost always acknowledged that life on earth was not fair. Hence, the need to look forward to a time and a place where love, compassion, and justice were found in abundance.

As I studied in detail the lyrics of these classic songs and hymns, I also realized something profound and inspiring. While they point toward an eternal life in heaven, almost all of them spell out ways to bring a bit of heaven to earth. In other words, they are less about the ultimate rewards of a Christian life well lived and more about how to live a Christian life in this world. In that way, these songs mirror the parables of Jesus and his charge found in Matthew 25:35–40 to reach out to the least of these.

As I edited and rewrote the stories behind these amazing marriages of lyrics and music, an image continued to knock on my mind's door: the famous jazz funerals of New Orleans. As they march to the cemetery, the mourners are accompanied by a solemn, slowly moving brass band playing songs such as "Just a Closer Walk with Thee," but as soon as they leave the gravesite, the musicians break into dance and blast out an up-tempo version of "When the Saints Go Marching In." So, yes, while the songs spotlighted in these pages do reflect on the heartbreak of separation, they also forecast a time of reunion and celebration. And that is something to get happy about.

Life is a challenge, life is a trial, and life is not fair, but for the Christian, there is another life where the books are balanced and love abounds. These are the musical stories of heaven as seen through the eyes of people who lived their faith on earth. These chapters offer a road map to making the journey to glory a bit easier and more fulfilling. They are also testimonies to the fact that there is a wonderful victory waiting just over the hilltop.

Author's note: When possible, the lyrics to these powerful songs and hymns are published with each story. For chapters where that is not possible, I suggest readers go online and review the lyrics at various hymn sites.

Wayfaring Stranger

A legal expert stood up to test Jesus. "Teacher," he said, "what must I do to gain eternal life?"

Jesus replied, "What is written in the Law? How do you interpret it?"

He responded, "You must love the Lord your God with all your heart, with all your being, with all your strength, and with all your mind, and love your neighbor as yourself."

Jesus said to him, "You have answered correctly. Do this and you will live."

But the legal expert wanted to prove that he was right, so he said to Jesus, "And who is my neighbor?"

Jesus replied, "A man went down from Jerusalem to Jericho. He encountered thieves, who stripped him naked, beat him up, and left him near death. Now it just so happened that a priest was also going down the same road. When he saw the injured man, he crossed over to the other side of the road and went on his way. Likewise, a Levite came by that spot, saw the injured man, and crossed over to the other side of the road and went on his way. A Samaritan, who was on a journey, came to where the man was. But when he saw him, he was moved with compassion. The Samaritan went to him and bandaged his wounds, tending them with oil and wine. Then he placed the wounded man on his own donkey, took him to an inn, and took care of him. The next day, he took two full days' worth of wages and gave them to the innkeeper. He said, 'Take care of him, and when I return, I will pay you back for any additional costs.' What do you think? Which one of these three was a neighbor to the man who encountered thieves?"

Then the legal expert said, "The one who demonstrated mercy toward him."

Jesus told him, "Go and do likewise."

Luke 10:25–37

I am a poor wayfaring stranger
Traveling through this world of woe.
There is no sickness, toil or danger
In that fair land to which I go.

I'm going home to see my mother,
I'm going home no more to roam;
I'm just a-going over Jordan,
I'm just a-going over home.

I know dark clouds will hover on me,
I know my pathway is rough and steep;
But golden fields lie out before me
Where weary eyes no more shall weep.

I'm going home to see my father,
I'm going home no more to roam;
I'm just a-going over Jordan,
I'm just a-going over home.

I'll soon be free from every trial,
This form shall rest beneath the sun.
I'll drop the cross of self-denial
And enter in that home with God.

*W*hen Jesus exposed the nature of prejudice in the parable of the good Samaritan, he likely revealed a picture of God that many in his audience had never seen. The God they thought they worshiped was a God of just one people. Those of different races or tribes were usually considered to be lesser beings and not a part of the Lord's plans. Not only was there no place for them in heaven, but they also were not to mix with the chosen ones while on earth. To have Jesus hold up the Samaritan as reflecting God's love, compassion, and grace must have been very sobering to many in that time and likely still is to this day. In a very real sense, this American folk song embraces a similar message but with a much different result.

There is no record of who wrote "Wayfaring Stranger." History proves that it has been around for at least two and a half centuries. It most assuredly originated in rural America. Some scholars have linked it to black spirituals, while others have tied it to Native American stories, but no matter its origins, there can be no doubt of its intent. It is a song that reveals a faith deeper than most could imagine and a challenge few were willing to accept.

Long before the term *blues* was invented, the person who penned "Wayfaring Stranger" understood what it was to be drowning in sorrow. Reading between the song's often depressing lines reveals a few obvious facts. The writer was likely poor, misunderstood, and homeless. It seems they were wandering because they were either lonely or lost. In a very real sense, the writer was a pilgrim engaged in a journey of searching. The unique thing about this pilgrimage was that the final destination—and the hope it would bring—could not be found on this earth.

According to the dictionary, *hopelessness* means having no expectation of good or success coming your way. Almost every line of "Wayfaring Stranger" screams out that the only thing waiting around the next bend is more sorrow, sadness, loneliness, and rejection. And yet, even though the writer expects nothing but pain on earth, there is a sense of hope found at the end of each verse. The suffering will not last! There is a place of acceptance and healing.

Over the past two centuries, "Wayfaring Stranger" has served as fodder for sermons, political speeches, and even charity fund-raisers. It has been sung in churches, on concert stages, in movies, on television shows, and in bars. In the 1940s, it became a hit for folksinger Burl Ives. During the

1960s, "Wayfaring Stranger" emerged as an anthem supporting integration and equal rights. Over the last fifty years, it has appeared on country, rock, popular, and religious charts and has been translated into more than fifty languages. Though "Wayfaring Stranger" is much younger than many well-known hymns, no song dealing with a pilgrim's journey to heaven has been sung by more people. So the question is, Why does its message still endure?

Throughout history, there have always been nomadic people. Some chose to wander, while others were forced by circumstance to continually move around. The common theme for both groups was the lack of means to settle down. Because of the insight found in the haunting lyrics, the author of "Wayfaring Stranger" might have been a victim of birth due to poverty or a disability or events beyond their control. As they traveled, they might have found little compassion or charity. Poor and destitute or blessed with deep empathy, they must have witnessed despair, disease, and hunger. They saw people treated as if they didn't matter. So in their travels, they observed a world that often revealed the worst of humanity.

Where "Wayfaring Stranger" moves from being a straight blues number and into a hymn that has inspired generations of people is its acknowledgment of grace. In spite of a lifetime of suffering and mistreatment, the author's faith did not waver. They still believe that God has reserved a home for them in heaven. And once they cross the Jordan,

15

they will be held in much higher esteem than those who reviled them.

On the surface, "Wayfaring Stranger" embraces a message only the poorest of the poor could relate to. It seems to be a song for the slave, refugee, and orphan. But in truth, even those who have been deeply blessed cannot escape all the heartaches of an earthly life. Therefore, in one way or another, the message found in "Wayfaring Stranger" is universal. The song's promise of a journey ending with being surrounded by loved ones is the ray of sunshine everyone can cling to. Yet "Wayfaring Stranger" is much more than a song that presents the rewards found in heaven. Viewing it that way misses the point the writer was likely trying to teach.

Just as Christ did with the parable of the good Samaritan, "Wayfaring Stranger" offers a challenge for the living. For most who wander the earth despondent and alone, as well as for those who have been abused or abandoned, all hope is dashed. These souls don't know the security of home or the promise found in faith. They have never felt a kind hand and rarely heard loving voices. So the only way they will ever meet God is to experience the grace of one who has already been blessed.

Christ touched the lepers when no one else would. Jesus invited a tax collector to dinner when everyone else avoided him. Story after story proves that much of the ministry of the Son of God dealt with wayfaring strangers. He didn't just offer them a ticket to heaven; he brought a bit of heaven down to earth and, in the process, revealed how God expected all his children to treat one another.

The person who penned "Wayfaring Stranger" has been experiencing the joys of heaven for a long time, and whenever this song is sung, the writer's wisdom and insight revisit earth and offer both a prayer of hope and a dynamic challenge. The prayer is that we each have the faith to endure the journey while maintaining our focus on God. The challenge is to love today's wanderers just as Christ did during his walk on earth. Grace brings us to heaven, and grace shared can bring heaven to the wayfaring stranger.

The Old Gospel Ship

We didn't bring anything into the world and so we can't take anything out of it: we'll be happy with food and clothing.

1 Timothy 6:7–8

I'm going to take a trip in that old gospel ship;
I'm a-going far beyond the sky.
I'm gonna shout and sing 'til heaven rings
When I bid this world goodbye.

I have good news to bring, and that is why I sing;
All my joys with you I'll share.
I'm going to take a trip in that old gospel ship
And go sailing through the air.

I can scarcely wait, I know I won't be late;
I'll spend my time in prayer.
And when the ship comes in, I'll leave this world
    of sin
And go sailing through the air.

If you are ashamed of me, you ought not to be;
Yes, you'd better have a care.
If too much fault you find, you will sure be left behind
While I'm sailing through the air.

*S*ometimes life can be an unfair struggle against forces that can't be understood or controlled. There are times when the weight of circumstances pins us down and demands we give up. Because the ultimate victory is assured to all who believe in Jesus, the rewards found in another place and another time can sustain us even when life seems hopeless. Nowhere is that clearer than when we consider the history behind one of gospel music's most optimistic and upbeat standards. It is a testament to this song's power that even before its writer's story was known, his message of eternal grace had delivered hope to millions.

"The Old Gospel Ship" is a spiritual anthem of joy. Via a recording pressed onto a ten-inch-wide, seventy-eight-rpm disk, the legendary Carter Family introduced this now familiar standard to fans of what was then called "hillbilly music." Now all but forgotten except by music historians and ardent country music fans, the Carters were a mountain folk trio who used rudimentary harmonies combined with guitar and autoharp accompaniments to frame the stories of life, loss, heartache, and faith found in the poverty of rural America. Their slow, almost plodding rendition of "The Old Gospel

Ship" served to introduce the standard to thousands suffering through the Great Depression. Thus, the singers' sober arrangement fit the mood of millions at the same time the uplifting lyrics offered some hope of better days to come. Still, unlike "Wildwood Flower" and "I'm Thinking Tonight of My Blue Eyes," this Carter record was not a hit. In fact, the hopeful anthem about heaven didn't garner much popularity until the LeFevre Family rode the musical ship up regional religious record charts about a decade later.

This new arrangement was much more upbeat than the Carters' and created such a stir that choir directors demanded choral arrangements of this version of "The Old Gospel Ship." Just before World War II, when the song finally appeared in songbooks, the LeFevres' patriarch, Alphus, was listed as the song's arranger. Wanting to give credit where credit was due, the Tennessee Music and Printing Company and the Stamps-Baxter Music and Printing Company asked LeFevre, who prided himself on knowing the stories behind almost every gospel song, who should get credit for writing "The Old Gospel Ship." Though he had been singing it since childhood, LeFevre admitted he had no idea who had penned the story of this unique ride to heaven. Thus, no one was given credit for a song that was now being sung by tens of thousands.

During the golden age of southern gospel music in the 1950s through the 1970s, the LeFevres' "Gospel Ship" served as an anchor for their live performances. Unlike many congregations that sang the old number to a slow, drawn-out tune, the LeFevres put wings to their music and performed it as if they were in a sprint. Just the first few notes of their up-tempo arrangement brought dead audiences to their feet. Though the LeFevres would introduce a dozen religious hits to American audiences, it was always "The Old Gospel Ship" that crowds demanded. Yet another family group would move the song to the status of a gospel classic.

The brothers and sisters who made up the Happy Goodmans had been performing together since World War II, but they emerged as an important family group only in the early 1960s. A decade later, after one of their key members, Vestal, almost died from a heart attack, the family embraced songs reflecting the realization that life was fragile and the only hope was found in faith. One night a trio of Goodman brothers sang a song that was not normally a part of their show. After the men finished a moderately paced rendition of "The Old Gospel Ship," Vestal surprised the audience by walking out and completing the number using a fast, dramatic, spirited arrangement, not unlike that employed by the LeFevres. It was as if heaven had come down to earth! The audience was so overjoyed to see the woman back on stage that they called her back for several encores of "The Old Gospel Ship." Vestal returned to the stage, and the Goodmans latched on to this solid old musical vessel at just the moment when southern gospel was exploding across the nation. This ancient song would become the group's signature number, and the Goodmans' version became so popular that soon everyone in the gospel music world was putting their spin on the song. It was even recorded by contemporary Christian, rock, folk, and country music acts.

The new popularity of "The Old Gospel Ship" prompted a host of music historians to dig into the song's roots. When they uncovered the song's humble origins, they also gained a deeper appreciation for the hopeful testimony found in the lyrics.

The story of this song did not originate in American music. It actually began in Africa. The song's writer had once roamed freely through jungles and across plains. Then slave traders captured him and many of his young friends and chained them together. First placed in a pen, they were then herded onto a ship like cattle. Confused and lost, they had no way of knowing they would never see their homes again.

For weeks, they were kept in the bow of the ship. If they cried out, they were whipped. Fed very little and placed in quarters so close they couldn't even lie down, over half of those who boarded the slave ship died. Their lifeless bodies were tossed into the ocean without so much as a prayer. For men who had once lived life running free in their homeland, this was a nightmare too disturbing to comprehend. At that time, none of them understood the meaning of the word *slave*, but for the rest of their lives, they would be nothing more than property.

In a strange world, the future songwriter found everything from the landscape to the language new to him. Frightened, alone, and caged like an animal, the young man was sure he would soon be killed. Yet instead, he was put on a stage, poked, prodded, examined, and sold. For the next two decades, he worked alongside hundreds of others on a large plantation. Though at night most of the African natives talked of freedom, the young man remained mute, sensing there was no hope. He would never return to his native land, never be able to choose what he did or have the chance to have a family, a home, or any possessions. Worst of all, though he could see beyond the bounds of the land his owner farmed, the man would not be able to explore the world around him. He would live and die a slave.

Legend has it that late in the slave's life, his owner determined that the African was too old to work in the cotton fields, so he was sold to another man. The new master built a church for his slaves and told them the story of Christ. And in that modest log building, the slave first heard the gospel story. Seeing Jesus as a brother and finding hope in the promise of freedom gained through death and resurrection, he became a Christian.

While there would be no escape from his earthly plight, the slave used his faith in the rewards of heaven to endure the torture of his existence. Over time, he began to picture a ship. Rather than bringing men to a life of slavery and pain, this ship took them to an eternity filled with freedom and joy. Setting his thoughts to music, he took his story of "The Old Gospel Ship" to the fields with him. He sang it for others, sharing with them the saving grace they could find only through Christ. Soon scores of voices were echoing the hope of these lyrics. The singers clung to the notion that while a ship might have brought them to a world of pain and suffering, another ship was coming to take them to a world filled with love and sunshine. As the men and women were sold to other owners and taken to other places, they took the song with them, and "The Old Gospel Ship" was handed down from generation to generation. Eventually, it was taught to Alphus LeFevre.

The song's writer will never be known by name, but the faith he found in the promise of heaven is still alive and blessing millions. Though most of us will thankfully never know what it is like to be sold on an auction block and have no freedom of choice, every person can relate to being bound and even held captive by worldly concerns, temptations, addictions, or fears. As the slave discovered, when people fully accept Christ, they are freed from a bit of the pain and suffering found in this life because they can see the better days that are just ahead. So all Christians, even in the worst of times, should be able to sing, "I have good news to bring!" And with their eyes on the prize, every Christian should also be able to realize that in true faith a bit of heaven, joy, and peace can be found as they wait to board the ship that will take them through the air to their eternal home.

To learn more, read Mylon LeFevre's autobiography, *Live Forever*, published by Heritage Builders in 2013.

If We Never Meet Again

Then, we who are living and still around will be taken up together with them in the clouds to meet with the Lord in the air. That way we will always be with the Lord.

1 Thessalonians 4:17

Perhaps there is no fear as great as that of being separated from loved ones. The challenge of going through life alone, with no one on your side, is simply over-whelming. Thus, it is natural that those who have been in our corners, supporting us through both thick and thin, become more than just friends and family. They are the foundation of who we are. We can't imagine life without them. And when we lose them to death, it is only expected that a part of us seems to die as well. Perhaps no song captures the emotions of loss better than one written in the midst of a world war. And while the lyrics found in "If We Never Meet Again" begin with a foreboding reminder of the inevitability of life

25

ending in death, they conclude with a powerful vision of a better day and life. Essentially, this song—penned by a master scribe who later related in his biography and his speeches that he found himself awash in an unexpected depression—builds a musical bridge from this world to the next.

Albert Brumley was born in Oklahoma in 1905 and began singing as a toddler. In his teens, he became a fully committed Christian who felt a call to share the gospel. At twenty, the slightly built man gave in to what many viewed as an immature dream and left his home state to travel to Arkansas to meet the South's greatest composer of contemporary hymns.

Eugene Bartlett was not expecting company. Brumley had neither written nor called before making the trek by train to Siloam Springs, Arkansas. So when an unfamiliar, travel-worn young man knocked on his door, the seasoned composer likely thought the poorly dressed guest was a salesman. In a way, he was, but the Oklahoman was not peddling goods; he was pitching talent. With a smile on his face, he begged Bartlett for a chance to study music at the master's feet. Immediately recognizing the gentle visitor's sincere desire to learn, the songwriter asked him into his home. Within a few hours, Bartlett was so deeply impressed by Brumley's enthusiasm that he invited him to stay in the guest room. At that time, Bartlett could not have guessed that by opening up his home to the stranger, he would set in motion a songwriting career that would see the young Oklahoman write more gospel standards than anyone in history.

For Brumley, Eugene Bartlett was more than a teacher; he became a mentor, friend, cheerleader, and spiritual father. While the established songwriter and publisher taught the young man the fundamentals of writing and business, the two prayed, ate, and worked together. The bond would last until Bartlett's death in 1941.

His education completed and using Bartlett's contacts, Brumley hit the road, displaying his singing abilities at concerts in one-room schoolhouses, churches, and revivals and on radio programs. While people loved to watch the young man perform, his ability to match emotions with lyrics defined his work and made him a gospel music star. During the Great Depression, he could relate to the plight of those he met during his performances. As he had grown up poor, he knew well the pains of hunger and hopelessness. But as a committed Christian, he also fully understood and believed in the power of faith. Through these contrasting experiences rooted in both hopelessness and hope, he was able to take human pessimism and Christian optimism and weave them together in songs that truly captured the mood of desperate people and the grace of a risen Savior. Using this formula and usually employing three short stanzas, Brumley preached some of the greatest sermons ever heard. Because his upbeat music matched his optimistic message, those who listened to his hymns usually left singing them as well. Thus, long after he had moved on to another town, his thoughts were still touching souls through the voices of others.

Due to the economic downturn that hit America beginning in 1929, Brumley was singing to crowds who had lost everything. The people he met were desperately poor and drowning in insecurity. While they deeply appreciated his work, they had nothing but smiles to give him. Driven only by the encouragement of friends and his faith, Brumley fought the odds and kept going. Yet it would be almost a decade before the songwriter sold enough of his music to finally climb out of the pit of poverty. Perhaps this is the reason Brumley lingered to meet every man, woman, and child who came to his performances. He wanted to do more than thank them for listening to him; he wanted to look into their hearts, feel their needs, share their joys, and get to know them individually. He needed them to realize that he was experiencing their pain and to show them there were better days coming. From these one-on-one meetings, Brumley drew much of the inspiration for his work.

For most of his adult life, Brumley had an intense schedule. For months at a time, he appeared nightly in tabernacles, brush arbors, churches, auditoriums, theaters, and stadiums. Perhaps because of the gypsy-like nature of his chosen life, Brumley knew the sad reality of meeting people, making ties, and then moving on. As time passed, the many meetings and venues began to blur in his memory. When World War II broke out in Europe, a more profound realization of the transitory nature of relationships pushed the once optimistic composer into a dark, depressive state. Now

Brumley couldn't look into a crowd without seeing the faces of young men who might soon be fighting for their lives on a distant battlefield. Beside them he saw sweethearts and wives, mothers, fathers, brothers, sisters, and even children who would soon know the anguish of uncertain separation and perhaps the cold reality of death. Though he constantly prayed it wouldn't happen, he felt war was coming to the United States.

In 1941, when America entered the war and young men boarded ships and planes headed for uncertain futures, Brumley's thoughts of separation, thoughts of never having another reunion with each new audience, and the very realization that many in the crowds might soon die began to haunt his dreams. Death had never seemed so real and so final. And for a while, all thoughts of heaven eluded a man whose faith was finally being fully tested.

The unexpected death of his mentor and biggest cheer-leader, Eugene Bartlett, really put the fragility of life into stark focus. Brumley wasn't ready to bid farewell to his old friend. He still had too much he needed to share with Bartlett. This passing put the songwriter into a deep spiral.

When praying for guidance and strength didn't seem to work, Brumley was driven to sit down with pen in hand and try to put into words the emotions of his heart. Surprisingly, his seemingly convoluted thoughts spilled easily from his head and fell into verses. With very little effort, seemingly guided by the Lord himself, Brumley wrote the stanzas and a chorus to a new song. As he studied where his doubts and faith met in music, he realized he had composed an anthem not just for his own needs but for the needs of millions of others as well.

Within weeks, he had arranged his new composition for churches and choirs, published it through his own company, and sung it scores of times on the radio and in concerts. Within a year, "If We Never Meet Again" had become one of the most popular hymns in the nation. For the remainder of the war, the song Brumley had written to regain his own faith was sung in thousands of churches as a promise of a great reunion coming in the future: "I will meet you on that beautiful shore," he sang.

Albert Brumley never considered himself an artist. He never thought of his verses as ranking with the works of Shakespeare or Mark Twain. He was just a simple storyteller who set his views to elementary melodies and arrangements. Still, his modest but inspired lyrics spoke to the hearts of both rich and poor. Men and women who were on a spiritual quest found answers in his text. Many who had never even considered coming to the Lord met Jesus for the first time in Brumley's compositions.

During World War II, his song "If We Never Meet Again" brought solace and comfort to a nation at war. Yet even after the fighting ended and most of the sons, husbands, and fathers came home to their families, the gospel hymn continued to provide a lifeline for those who had lost loved ones.

It remains popular today because it is more about life than death, more about coming together than being separated by distance or time. In reality, "If We Never Meet Again" is Christian faith taken to a higher level of understanding by three simple stanzas and a gentle chorus. It is a promise for a future when there will be no separation, no mourning, no loss, and no heartache but a reunion in which those who supported us, believed in us, cheered for us, and encouraged us can be thanked for their love and grace. It is a song that assures each Christian that we will meet again in another place and another time and that no goodbye lasts forever and no farewell is final. In a world of darkness and pain, "If We Never Meet Again" brings hope and light.

Amazing Grace

The people were amazed and said, "What kind of person is this? Even the winds and the lake obey him!"

Matthew 8:27

Amazing grace! How sweet the sound
That saved a wretch like me!
I once was lost, but now am found;
Was blind, but now I see.

'Twas grace that taught my heart to fear,
And grace my fears relieved;
How precious did that grace appear
The hour I first believed.

Through many dangers, toils and snares,
I have already come;
'Tis grace hath brought me safe thus far,
And grace will lead me home.

The Lord has promised good to me,
His Word my hope secures;
He will my Shield and Portion be,
As long as life endures.

Yea, when this flesh and heart shall fail,
And mortal life shall cease,
I shall possess, within the veil,
A life of joy and peace.

The earth shall soon dissolve like snow,
The sun forbear to shine;
But God, who called me here below,
Will be forever mine.

When we've been there ten thousand years,
Bright shining as the sun,
We've no less days to sing God's praise
Than when we first begun.

In Matthew 8, the power of Jesus is clearly displayed in only five verses. Scripture shows that while Christ was able to calmly sleep as the winds and rain raged, the disciples were so badly shaken that they feared for their lives. When the frightened men finally approached Jesus, he got up, went up on deck, and simply told the winds to go away. Within seconds, the storm was stilled and those sailing with Christ were once more secure.

In our lives, there are many times when once small situations become storms and grow to threaten us on every side. We want peace but can't seem to find it. Just like the disciples, when our world is rocked, we tend to panic. We lose sleep and struggle for answers. Ironically, as we try to control our fate, we often fail to turn to the one who holds the whole world in his hands.

Like the disciples, another man of the sea once found himself in the midst of a storm. This natural calamity led to a despicable soul turning to God and set in motion events leading to the creation of the world's most beloved hymn. It is still sobering to note that "Amazing Grace" was born not from an experience of love but from a sordid tale of human exploitation, and that this exploitation did not stop when salvation was given but continued for several more years. To fully appreciate "Amazing Grace," one must know the full story behind it and understand that the hymn's writer wasn't saved from just one storm . . . his entire life was a storm.

John Newton was born in London, England, on August 4, 1725. Though not a product of poverty, Newton did not have a wonderful or secure home life. His father was a hardened sailor and was often gone for months at a time. While Mrs. Newton was a loving Christian woman, a devoted parent who took a vital interest in her son, she was also chronically ill and physically weak. Because of his mother's frailty and his father's absence, Newton, from the time he could walk, literally had the run of the house. He was just seven when his mother died. Four years later, the child followed in his father's footsteps and became a cabin boy on a ship.

Even before his teens, Newton was a hard-drinking and ill-tempered lad. Law officers in port towns called the youth vicious, brutal, and void of empathy. His demeanor was so violent and unpredictable that he even scared veteran sailors. By the time he was twenty, he had spilled more blood than most career soldiers and consumed enough alcohol to stock London's largest pub. He later described himself as a godless monster, and few who knew him during his youth would have disagreed. In a profession that attracted the worst kind of people, Newton was in a class by himself.

He was running from the law when he fled Europe and landed in Sierra Leone. In this African nation, Newton discovered sailors who matched him in depravity. In the quest for money, Newton and his shipmates traded guns, spices, liquor, and clothes for souls. This human cargo was taken to an old ship, and more than six hundred people were chained shoulder to shoulder in the ship's hold. Once they were secure, Newton and his comrades set sail for America. During the next six weeks, about 40 percent of the captives died. Those who somehow survived the torturous journey were then sold at auctions, with a portion of the proceeds ending up in Newton's pockets. Now awash in cash, the sailor urged his new friends to head back to Africa to collect more spoils. Newton would happily continue this horrific practice for years.

In most ports, slavers were much lower on the human chain than even pirates. Thus, Newton was not welcome in anyone's home and was even reviled by most churches. Some preachers declared that those who plied the slave trade were too far gone to save. But as long as he had money for liquor and women, Newton didn't care what the world thought.

Newton's decadent life was fueled by America's addiction to slavery. Ironically, many of the men who bought Newton's cargo were Christians who found biblical ways to justify their actions. The moral indifference displayed by most in the established churches made it easier for Newton to thrive. To him, black humans were just soulless products to use and dispose of. As Newton numbly tossed dead men and women overboard, or watched others being sold on auction blocks, his hardened heart was not touched.

The weeks spent crossing the Atlantic offered sailors plenty of free time. In 1758, on a trip from Africa to America, twenty-three-year-old Newton looked through the ship's few books and found *The Imitation of Christ*. Looking for a way to pass the time, he picked it up and began to leaf through the pages. As the hours passed, the slaver began to consider the role of Christ in the world. Only when dark clouds appeared and winds began jostling the ship's masts did Newton finally look up and realize the slave ship was heading directly into a hurricane. Because it was too late to change course, the men and their cargo would have to ride it out. Putting the book to one side, Newton went to work lashing down provisions and supplies.

Within an hour, the ship was rolling back and forth, and thousands of gallons of water drenched the frightened men. While those around him cried, cursed, and begged, Newton thought back on his own miserable life. The sailor concluded that the only person he had ever known who had really loved him was his mother. He also realized that she would be heartbroken if she knew what he had become. Remembering a prayer he had once heard her pray, he fell to his knees. With the rain pelting down, Newton promised that if God would give him a second chance, he would become a moral man.

In a matter of minutes, the storm abated and roared off to the east. Miraculously, not one person lost their life that day, and the mildly damaged ship was able to complete its journey. For the first time, when Newton was given his cut of the profits, he did not seek out a pub to celebrate. Instead, the man who had felt the touch of God's saving hand returned to his ship to read. It seemed to those around him that the sailor had gone soft. But while he had given up drinking and fighting, his moral compass was still not set. He continued in the slave trade and within two years had his own ship. As a captain, he oversaw human cargo from capture to the auction blocks. Yet now the deaths of captives ate at him, as did the money he was given to deliver the young Africans to their future owners. It was as if he was being haunted by Jesus.

On a layover in England, Newton sought out Charles Wesley. Over the course of several weeks, the famous father of the Methodist movement convinced the sailor to finally and fully acknowledge his sins. After his confession, Newton gave up his profession along with a lifetime of bad habits and accepted a call to preach. But like the apostle Paul, the now ex-slaver couldn't fully escape his past. From time to time, it still came back to tap him on the shoulder.

In 1779, two decades after he was literally and spiritually saved, Newton was pastoring a church in Olney, England. As he read the account of the storm detailed in Matthew 8, Newton came to understand that this story was not about just one night and one storm; it was about the unpredictable nature of life itself. So the fear the disciples displayed was found in every person on the face of the globe. With this realization in mind, he wrote a message on grace. From the pulpit, the now respected moral voice and beloved community leader cited the storm that had once scared the disciples. He then shocked his congregation with his life story of how the Lord had come to him during a violent storm. He finished his message by singing a self-penned song that began with these touching but now forgotten words.

> In evil long I took delight,
> Unawed by shame or fear.
> Till a new object struck my sight,
> And stopped my wild career.

Newton's "Amazing Grace" may have been composed for a single sermon, but it quickly made its way into songbooks. The hymn first gained wide acceptance in the American South. Little did those in slave states realize that the song had been inspired by a man's realization of the immorality of the very thing that was sustaining the southern economy. It was also in the United States that Newton's verses were published in the songbook *Kentucky Harmony*. The tune became the musical vehicle that transported Newton's personal testimony across a new frontier and then back to England. Today, the tune most often used with Newton's lyrics is called "New Britain."

Newton's hymn was about salvation and living a Christian life. It spoke of the freedom that faith offered in a world rife with sin. It talked about the life-sustaining joy and comfort in following the example of Christ. But the rewards of eternal life were only alluded to in Newton's final verse, and heaven was not mentioned. So how did "Amazing Grace" become a great song forecasting the joy of eternal life?

In the early 1800s, an unknown American writer penned another verse to "Amazing Grace." This stanza spoke of the promise and the joy that would be found in heaven. When these lines were added to previously published verses, the hymn seemed complete.

> When we've been there ten thousand years,
> Bright shining as the sun,

We've no less days to sing God's praise
Than when we first begun.

John Newton's "Amazing Grace" was written as a musical road map showing how to seek forgiveness and then explaining what that forgiveness can mean to the past, present, and future. Still, it took another man to realize that Newton's hymn lacked one vital element of the Christian story of grace and faith. This new, final verse pointed out that heaven is a place where there are no storms. It is a destination where a calm peace reigns not just for a day but forever.

If he were here today, Newton would likely remind us that in looking toward the tranquility of heaven, we must not forget what the disciples learned that night during the storm. Jesus can bring peace to our lives on earth if we turn our storms over to him. So by calling on Christ, we get to have a little heaven on earth too.

To learn more about the fascinating life of John Newton, read Jonathan Aitken's *John Newton: From Disgrace to Amazing Grace*, published by Crossway in 2007.

Can [Will] the Circle Be Unbroken?

After this I looked, and there was a great crowd that no one could number. They were from every nation, tribe, people, and language. They were standing before the throne and before the Lamb. They wore white robes and held palm branches in their hands.

Revelation 7:9

There are loved ones in the glory
Whose dear forms you often miss.
When you close your earthly story,
Will you join them in their bliss?

In the joyous days of childhood
Oft they told of wondrous love
Pointed to the dying Saviour;
Now they dwell with Him above.

You remember songs of heaven
Which you sang with childish voice.
Do you love the hymns they taught you,
Or are songs of earth your choice?

You can picture happy gath'rings
Round the fireside long ago,
And you think of tearful partings
When they left you here below.

One by one their seats were emptied.
One by one they went away.
Now the family is parted.
Will it be complete one day?

Will the circle be unbroken
By and by, by and by?
Is a better home awaiting
In the sky, in the sky?

*D*ue to the imperfect nature of the world, humans are often conflicted when it comes to dealing with even those people who should be closest to them in mind and spirit. As Paul alluded to in 1 Corinthians 13, in this world, we don't always see things clearly. Relationships are often strained by immature jealousy, envy, misunderstanding, and greed. So the promise of the next life is of a world where human frailties will be erased and replaced by a wisdom that will "clothe" us all with complete understanding. Petty things that create friction in relationships on earth will not encumber heavenly reunions. Without this strain, the circle of life will be not only complete but also perfect. And that is the basis for a song that speaks of a hope that distressed families will once more be united through the bonds of unflawed love.

In the early days of our nation's history, the American upper class may have listened to the classical music of Europe, but the rural settlers were revising English folk music and adapting it to their lives. In a very real sense, this rural music, sung in both homes and churches, became an oral history of tragedy, suffering, hope, and faith. It was also a way of connecting with homes and loved ones far across the sea. And through music, questions were asked about everything from love to loss to life to death.

A. P. Carter was one of many early recording artists who sought out obscure folk songs for performance material. Employing ancient English tunes updated with uniquely American lyrics, the Carter Family had a string of country music hits in the 1920s. In 1935, the breakup of A. P. and Sara's marriage left a shaken A. P. He was leafing through a songbook and came across "Will the Circle Be Unbroken?" Written by Ada R. Habershon and Charles H. Gabriel in 1907, the song framed a promised grand reunion through the gift of salvation.

Carter took the heart of the chorus found in "Will the Circle Be Unbroken?" and worked in his own ideas for new stanzas. When he was finished, he had changed the song's title and tagline to "Can the Circle Be Unbroken?" Likely due to his recent divorce and the impact of the Great Depression, he had also penned new verses that painted a much darker picture of the toll created by separation and death. These lyrics were not of sweet memories but of the oppressive sense of loss that gathered like dark clouds when a loved one died. In each stanza, heartbroken souls who had come together to say goodbye to a loved one were questioning why death had entered their lives. As the verses progressed, the mourners' cries grew louder, and they demanded to know if their family circle would, from this day forth, remain broken. In a very real sense, the new song was as haunting as an Edgar Allan Poe short story, but thanks to the chorus, it was also much more hopeful.

If Carter had intended for the message found in "Can the Circle Be Unbroken?" to sway Sara to come back to him, the song failed. While the lyrics might not have swayed his ex-wife, they did move millions of country music fans. This folk anthem, about a man burying his beloved mother and those who had gathered at the funeral to say goodbye, struck a chord. In fact, at a time when the Great Depression was raging, millions could identify with the crushing weight of doubt and loss, and in the midst of their grief, they needed assurance that all would be well in the future. Carter's song gave them both sides of life's coin—the helplessness and the promise. So while it might have been about a funeral, it was also about a victory.

"Can the Circle Be Unbroken?" was a huge seller in the rural South and Midwest, and at least a part of the reason had to be the climate of suffering and insecurity then engulfing the American landscape. Across the nation, families were being torn apart by poverty and despair. Drowning in debt, millions had packed up their belongings and moved across America looking for work. For these homeless and nomadic refugees, Carter's new take on the old hymn became a personal statement of faith.

As with all hits, "Can the Circle Be Unbroken?" stayed on radio playlists for a few months and then slowly drifted out of commercial music. But it was not completely forgotten. Carter's "Can the Circle Be Unbroken?" found new life in churches, revivals, and all-night singings. For the next two decades, it was one of the most sung hymns in the rural South, and only as the Great Depression became a distant memory did "Can the Circle Be Unbroken?" begin to fade from the Christian world as it had earlier from country music.

In 1968, rock 'n' roll pioneer Carl Perkins was a part of the *Johnny Cash Show*. Cash had given his old Sun Records label mate a job to pull Perkins out of an almost fatal addiction to drugs and alcohol. The man who had written such hits as "Blue Suede Shoes" used this second chance to embrace a deep commitment to his Christian faith. Back in an environment of grace, Perkins hit the road with Cash and in the process got to know A. P. Carter's daughter Maybelle. She had formed a new version of the Carter Family with her daughters. It became a habit that before and after shows, Perkins and the Carters would sing old country and gospel classics. One night while waiting in his dressing room, Perkins began to play around with a new idea built on a Carter gospel classic he had recently sung with Maybelle. "Daddy Sang Bass" borrowed a theme found in "Can the Circle Be Unbroken?" and combined it with the old American tradition of families singing together. When recorded by Johnny Cash, this new song stayed on the top of the country charts for six weeks—and more than just selling millions of records, it also revived interest in A. P.'s old hymn. "Can the Circle Be Unbroken?" was once more picked up by church congregations and gospel music groups. It also found its way back to funeral services.

By 1972, the Nitty Gritty Dirt Band had already produced a number of top pop hits, yet they surprised everyone when they broke the rock music mold and traveled to Nashville to team with country music legends Roy Acuff, Doc Watson, Earl Scruggs, Merle Travis, and Maybelle Carter for an album saluting traditional American folk music. The cuts from this recording session reawakened both the public and the industry to a classic country musical art form and in the process made "Can [Will] the Circle Be Unbroken?" the best-known country-gospel song of all time. Suddenly, it seemed everyone was singing this classic Christian hymn. It even became a hit in Europe and Asia.

The lyrics found in both versions of "Can [Will] the Circle Be Unbroken?" would have spoken just as clearly to early Christians as they did to Americans during the Great Depression. It is easy to see how the song's message could have

46

served as an anchor when Jesus commissioned his disciples. These eleven might be separated in their earthly missions, but in heaven, they and the circle would once again be united.

"Can [Will] the Circle Be Unbroken?" also would have resonated with men and women sixteen hundred years later who would leave Europe and come to the New World. The promise of a future reunion with the loved ones they left behind would have brought them hope and comfort.

Today, refugees all over the globe are facing severe separation anxiety. They are leaving behind everything they know and going to places with only a hope and a prayer as guidance. They realize the full weight of circles having been not just broken but shattered. If they heard "Can [Will] the Circle Be Unbroken?" it would no doubt speak to the questions they are asking.

The Bible reveals that soon after Jesus died, those who had known him in life recognized him after his resurrection. He was not a stranger to them. Logic therefore dictates that in heaven we will know our friends and families. And in heaven, when the circle is fully completed and all the broken elements of earth are left behind, the reunion will be as perfect as the life of the one who died to enable the circle to finally be unbroken.

Many books spotlight the work of the Carter Family. One of the more recent is Charles Hirshberg's *Will You Miss Me When I'm Gone? The Carter Family and Their Legacy in American Music*, published by Simon & Schuster in 2004.

When We All Get to Heaven

Clap your hands, all you people! Shout joyfully to God with a joyous shout!

Psalm 47:1

Sing the wondrous love of Jesus,
Sing His mercy and His grace;
In the mansions bright and blessed
He'll prepare for us a place.

Refrain:
When we all get to heaven,
What a day of rejoicing that will be!
When we all see Jesus,
We'll sing and shout the victory!

While we walk the pilgrim pathway,
Clouds will overspread the sky;

But when trav'ling days are over,
Not a shadow, not a sigh.

Let us then be true and faithful,
Trusting, serving every day;
Just one glimpse of Him in glory
Will the toils of life repay.

Onward to the prize before us!
Soon His beauty we'll behold;
Soon the pearly gates will open;
We shall tread the streets of gold.

In the two thousand years since Christ walked the earth, thousands of denominations have spun off from the first church. With each of those divisions, Christians have built walls between worshipers based on everything from different interpretations of certain Scripture passages, to the order of services, to the use of varying translations of the Bible, to the type of baptism used. Sometimes these seemingly trivial differences have created friction between believers, and at other times, they have led to wars. In these same houses of worship, so divided by doctrine and point of view, most teach that when our days on earth are finished and we are transported to heaven, it will be a time of joy and celebration when *all* those saved by grace will celebrate in unison.

A century and a half ago, things were not much different than they are today or a thousand years ago. People were divided along congregational lines, and the various groups rarely if ever mixed together in worship. More often than not, different churches were rivals rather than partners in sharing the gospel message. One of the exceptions was a product of the great revival movement of the late 1800s. At these tent meetings, bridges were built and walls disappeared as Congregationalists and Baptists shared hymnals with Methodists and Episcopalians, and they all raised their voices together in songs of praise. At one of these gatherings in the 1890s, where the emphasis was not on dogma or doctrine but on faith, a retired Presbyterian schoolteacher met a Methodist preacher's wife. That chance meeting sparked a friendship that led to the creation of one of the greatest songs of spiritual reunion ever penned. But long before that collaboration took place, one of the composers would have her faith tested in such a way that would end her career and plunge her into a world of intense pain.

Eliza Hewitt was born on June 28, 1851, in Pennsylvania. Her parents saw God as having no favorites. In their minds, the poor were as important as the rich, the black man was equal to the white, and women had as much value as men. Thus, the Hewitts taught their daughter to read, question, and think and to see herself not as a second-class citizen but as a creation of God who had no limits. Her parents drove her to excel in her studies, and at each level of education, she finished at the top of her class in the public school she attended.

In line with their thinking on academics, the Hewitts felt that a Christian must continue to grow in knowledge and faith. It was their belief that everyone had a calling. They preached that being more like Christ meant finding areas of service. Upon graduation, Eliza Hewitt seized on this element of her parents' faith and became a teacher.

As she entered a classroom filled with students who were transitioning from childhood to their teens, Hewitt was filled with a determination to shape her charges into modern men and women who would change the world. Each girl and boy was vitally important to her because they represented God's creation. In that way, they were a part of her family. She dedicated her work to giving them the same positive outlook and drive her parents had instilled in her. By all reports, Hewitt was a teacher who inspired even children who had once shown nothing but disdain for school. On most days, her classroom was a happy place. But in one moment, Hewitt's career, life, and even faith were challenged in ways she never could have imagined.

While Hewitt was attempting to discipline a ruggedly built teen, the angry boy took his slate and struck her. The attack sent her to the floor, and with scores of frightened eyes looking on, she could not rise. The blow so badly injured Hewitt that she was not able to walk. The teacher, barely in her twenties, was now an invalid. With one blow, she went from playing with her students during recess to not being able to get out of bed.

Her doctors doubted she would ever walk again, but Hewitt refused to give up. Six months later, though the act left her in agony, she pushed herself out of bed and took a few steps. Each day saw her take a few more, and over the course of months, she was finally able to leave her parents' home. Soon she established a routine. After her short daily excursions, she immersed herself in Bible study, filling notebooks with pages of observations and questions. Why had God allowed this to happen? Why had she been stripped of the thing she enjoyed most—teaching? Why was she now fated to live a life of isolation while battling constant pain? She found no answers.

As time crawled by, Hewitt thirsted to see more of the world. Because her back made long trips impossible, the lonely woman began to attend local revivals and camp meetings. Sitting on hard pews and benches brought searing pain, but in these cross-denominational gatherings, she sang, worshiped, and finally had the chance to visit with people again. The darkness that had crowded into her life as she suffered alone in her bed was replaced by fresh relationships. And these relationships led to a new calling.

Now when she was home alone, rather than feeling sorry for herself, she began to write poems to teach others how to survive disappointment and pain. When, in 1887, her poetic testimony was matched to music written by James Robson Sweney and became one of the greatest hymns of the revival movement, she found a new career. After "There Is Sunshine in My Soul Today," Hewitt's next popular song was "More about Jesus," followed by "My Faith Has Found a Resting

Place." Each of these Christian standards displayed elements of Hewitt's quest to control pain, suffering, and disappointment by immersing herself in a joyful relationship with the Savior. As her songs were published, thousands clung to Hewitt's hymns as if they were life rafts. Yet it would take a meeting with the songwriter Fanny Crosby to trigger an idea that bridged the gap between this life and the next.

In Crosby, Hewitt found someone who could readily identify with her pain. Crosby was blind. With her life limited by her disability, the songwriter had turned to the Bible for answers. What she had discovered was the joy found in worship and the hope of healing in heaven. With Crosby's inspirational example driving her, Hewitt began a poem reflecting her own tragic story. When that project didn't have the positive message she wanted, she moved from considering just her own life to digging into her experiences during worship. The more she considered the experiences she had when denominational walls were removed at tent meetings, the more she felt as though she was getting a glimpse of what heaven must be like.

In the initial verse of her new poem, she borrowed from the fourteenth chapter of John. She quoted the disciple's words on the guaranteed promise of a life that embraced faith. "In the mansions bright and blessed, he'll prepare for us a place." In four lines, she added that the way to gain entrance to heaven was to reflect the mercy and grace extended by Jesus. Thus, Hewitt painted a full picture of salvation and its rewards.

As she moved to the next verse, she drew from the book of Revelation. Likely inspired by her own plight and pain, as well as by Fanny Crosby's blindness, she first described the trials of an earthly life and contrasted them with the hope of a time when there would be no worries or complaints. When the storm clouds were gone, the struggles of an earthly life would be over. No doubt this optimistic view was also a product of what she experienced at camp meetings.

Next, much as if she were still in the classroom, she became a teacher giving a lesson on the rewards of playing by the rules and the Christian's need to seek and to serve. This was the philosophy she had learned from her parents, and now she had the chance to share it with the world. "Let us then be true and faithful, trusting, serving every day." And for Hewitt, serving meant more than just prayer; it meant using one's talents to lift others up. She was echoing Jesus when he asked each person to reach the least of these. And as a woman who had to struggle with pain each day, she knew what it was like to be one of those in need of help, comfort, and grace.

In the last verse, Hewitt again embraced her determination not to devalue her worth or potential in the face of crippling pain. She revealed this by showing the great rewards of striving to live a life to its fullest and in the process inspiring others to follow in her footsteps. In this verse, she explained that faith offered not just a way to get through bad times; there was a prize waiting for each one who had the strength to believe and endure.

The clincher to her poem was the chorus. Dying meant victory because it allowed Christians to come together as believers without walls. So, as in the worship found at the camp meetings, in the next life, dogma, politics, and position would be forgotten and replaced by the joy found in Christian acceptance and reunion. In her words and in her faith, Hewitt believed there was nothing to compare to the gathering of souls with Jesus.

Hewitt gave her poem to a friend she had met at a Christian conference in Ocean Grove, New Jersey. Emily Wilson was a composer and the wife of a Methodist minister. Wilson saw the wonder in Hewitt's lyrics and quickly created a tune matching the words' hope, enthusiasm, and joy. The song was soon published and, as per Hewitt's prayer, accepted by denominations around the globe.

For the final two decades of Eliza Hewitt's life, her crowning glory would be knowing that millions found inspiration in "When We All Get to Heaven," a song that could not have been written had she not experienced a life of pain and years of loneliness. She had taken a negative and transformed it into a positive message of faith.

Faith should unite Christians, not divide us. Our final reunion will be special, but by coming together in faith with other Christians on a regular basis, by casting aside differences in dogma or doctrine, we have the opportunity to bring heaven down to earth now and to have a vivid preview of that future day when we will sing and shout the victory.

Face to Face

I turned to see who was speaking to me, and when I turned, I saw seven oil lamps burning on top of seven gold stands. In the middle of the lampstands I saw someone who looked like the Human One. He wore a robe that stretched down to his feet, and he had a gold sash around his chest. His head and hair were white as white wool—like snow—and his eyes were like a fiery flame. His feet were like fine brass that has been purified in a furnace, and his voice sounded like rushing water. He held seven stars in his right hand, and from his mouth came a sharp, two-edged sword. His appearance was like the sun shining with all its power. When I saw him, I fell at his feet like a dead man. But he put his right hand on me and said, "Don't be afraid. I'm the first and the last, and the living one. I was dead, but look! Now I'm alive forever and always. I have the keys of Death and the Grave."

Revelation 1:12–18

Face to face with Christ, my Savior,
Face to face—what will it be,
When with rapture I behold Him,
Jesus Christ who died for me?

Refrain:
Face to face I shall behold Him,
Far beyond the starry sky;
Face to face in all His glory,
I shall see Him by and by!

Only faintly now I see Him,
With the darkened veil between,
But a blessed day is coming,
When His glory shall be seen.

What rejoicing in His presence,
When are banished grief and pain;
Death is swallowed up in vict'ry,
And the dark things shall be plain.

Face to face—oh, blissful moment!
Face to face—to see and know;
Face to face with my Redeemer,
Jesus Christ who loves me so.

In the fame-driven world we call home, most people experience a sense of awe when they meet a well-known celebrity. The moment when an average person has a chance to actually look into the eyes of a star and speak to them sparks a memory that few ever forget. Many years later, the memory of that meeting is still fresh.

What would it have been like to view Jesus face-to-face? What would it have been like to look into his eyes and hear his voice? How would such a meeting affect a person at that moment and for the rest of their life?

We will not get the chance to see Jesus in the flesh during our time on earth. We will have no opportunities to actually speak to him, ask questions, and listen to his responses. In fact, the only way for us to meet Jesus is through death, unless he comes back first. And if meeting Jesus is the reward for death, then leaving this world is really something to celebrate rather than to mourn.

As we read biblical accounts of those who knew Jesus, those who talked and walked with him, we are left with a picture that is incomplete. Except for John's words in Revelation describing the Christ of the rapture, none of the first-person accounts written by those who called Jesus friend provide a description of Christ. We don't know his height, his build, his eye color, or the shape of his face. We don't know how his voice sounded, how he walked, or the way he moved his hands when he spoke. But what these first-person accounts lack in physical description they make up for in other ways.

Time and time again the Gospel writers describe people's reactions to Jesus. From these encounters, we know that he was gentle but strong. He was able to challenge without attacking. As we read deeper, we discover that he often answered questions with questions. Therefore, Jesus was someone who forced people to look at themselves. And perhaps most importantly, Jesus was approachable. People were not so awed by his miracles that they felt they couldn't speak to him. And that was likely because his message focused not on power or wealth but on love and kindness.

On January 22, 1855, Carrie Ellis was born in Walden, Vermont. She was the second of seven children. After spending her first eight years in New England, her family moved to New Jersey. Her father, a farmer, was a devout Christian and made sure his family was in the pews at the local Presbyterian church several times a week. During those worship services, the bright and bubbly Carrie often raised her voice in song only to have a host of family members plead with her to keep her mouth closed. Sadly, the girl who so loved music was completely tone deaf and couldn't find a note to save her life.

Though she could not sing, Carrie could write. By her teens, she had penned countless poems. Her teachers were initially impressed by the student's grasp of meter and pacing, but over time, the humor and depth found in her writings made the greatest impact. One of her poems, "Washing Dishes," was published in the *Youth's Companion*. The thrill of seeing her work published pushed Carrie's desire to be an author. While none of her following verses found their way into print, one poem moved a local businessman to the point that he asked for Carrie's hand in marriage. On May

28, 1884, at the age of twenty-nine, the woman who many believed might end up an old maid wed Frank Breck.

Breck was in the grape business. Specifically, he made and sold juice. With a ready income, her husband offered Carrie security that many did not know. She never had to work outside the home or fear for a lack of food, but that didn't mean she was idle. Over the course of the next decade, she gave birth to five daughters, and caring for those girls and doing her household chores kept the woman so busy that she barely had any time to devote to her passion: composing poetry. She later explained that she simply couldn't give up writing, so she found ways to work it into her daily schedule.

"It [writing] was a great joy to me," she told songwriter Charles H. Gabriel, "and, as opportunity offered, I penciled verse under all sorts of conditions—over a mending basket, with a baby in arms, and sometimes even when sweeping or washing dishes, my mind moved to meter."[1]

Carrie's was a life set to a rhythm she couldn't explain in any way but through rhyme. And as this was the golden age of poetry, she was not alone in her passion. Books filled with poems were bestsellers, and at almost every public event, someone was asked to read a poem. In this environment, she nurtured a skill that would lead her to create a few simple verses that paved the way for hundreds of thousands to think of Christ as more than a historical figure; she would cast him as a Savior.

As her children grew, so did Carrie's thirst for understanding her faith. Thus, she spent time each night studying
the Bible. Sensing that believing in Jesus as a Redeemer was
not enough, she seized upon opportunities to help those who
were sick, destitute, or suffering. This drive to live like Christ
pushed her to pen a poem that paved the way for an unexpected opportunity. Feeling her verses offered a challenge
others might appreciate, she sent the poem off to the *Christian Herald*. Once the magazine found a composer to set it
to music, it was published. "You Ought to Do Something
for Jesus" became the first of more than a thousand songs
penned by Carrie. At the age of forty, almost three decades
after falling in love with writing, the tone-deaf woman had
a career.

In 1898, Carrie moved with her husband to Portland,
Oregon, and as her children were now older, she had more
time to devote to writing. As she studied new hymns, she
realized that the almost universal view of heaven was that it
was a place for joy and celebration. While she agreed that
the next life was one to embrace and anticipate with great
enthusiasm, she couldn't help dwelling on another facet of
crossing over the Jordan that most seemed to ignore.

For decades, Carrie had read biblical passages about Jesus
that had inspired her to write of Christ's love, death, and
resurrection. She had also penned heartfelt lyrics dealing
with his sacrifice. But there was another theme that kept
gnawing at her heart. As she considered this new point of

view, it both fascinated and frustrated her. She wondered what it would have been like to actually meet Jesus. The more she considered this vision, the more she felt heaven was not as much a resting place or a city filled with golden streets and huge homes as a place of illumination and gratitude. It was where Christians could say thank you to someone they knew but had never really met.

Carrie was very familiar with the story of the prodigal son. In a real sense, this parable reflected the drive behind her need to see Jesus face-to-face. The son in the story left home to live a life the father didn't approve of, and because of love, the father continued to look out from his front door each day waiting for that son to return to him. Realizing the error of his ways, the son humbled himself and made the long journey home. He had no idea what to expect and was surely shocked by the response of his father rushing to meet him with open arms.

With those thoughts in mind, Carrie penned three verses and a chorus and mailed it to her friend Grant Colfax Tullar. As soon as Tullar opened the envelope and read Carrie's "Face to Face," he went to his piano, threw away a set of lyrics he had just penned, and matched Carrie's poem with his new melody. This was a musical marriage made in heaven. Carrie had posed a question that longed to be answered and opened the door for people to see heaven as the place to meet Jesus face-to-face. Within a few years, "Face to Face" would become one of the most used invitation hymns in the world.

When writing about heaven, Carrie realized that the first and most important thing she would get to do there was see Jesus. He would be there to greet and welcome her to a reward she hadn't earned. When she left this world, Christ himself would open his arms and welcome her to a new, everlasting home. That vision, created by a tone-deaf woman, provided a pitch-perfect picture of Christ and the incredible greeting waiting for all when they arrive in heaven.

Roll, Jordan, Roll

If we have a hope in Christ only in this life, then we deserve to be pitied more than anyone else.

1 Corinthians 15:19

Went down to the river Jordan
Where John baptised three;
When I walked the devil in hell
Said "John ain't baptized me."

I said roll, Jordan, roll,
Roll, Jordan, roll.
My soul ought to rise in heaven, Lord,
For the year when Jordan rolls.

Well some say John was a Baptist,
Some say John was a Jew.
But I say John was a preacher
And my Bible says so too.

I said roll, Jordan, roll,
Roll, Jordan, roll.
My soul ought to rise in heaven, Lord,
For the year when Jordan rolls.

Hallelujah!

Roll, Jordan, roll,
Roll, Jordan, roll.
My soul ought to rise in heaven, Lord,
For the year when Jordan rolls.

*B*ecause the Bible is not specific when describing heaven, people have their own ideas as to what the hereafter looks like. One of the more universal themes in both sermons and songs is that people cross a river to get from this life to the next. That imagery likely hearkens back to one of the most monumental of all biblical stories: the children of Israel crossing the Jordan to get to the promised land. It is hardly surprising that in the 1700s and 1800s, American slaves closely identified with those once held in bondage in Egypt. It also seems natural that these slaves would take a song created by an early leader of the Methodist movement and convert it into a prayer focused on both heaven and freedom.

"Roll, Jordan, Roll" sprang to life in the fertile mind of Charles Wesley. Born in England in 1707, Charles was the younger brother of the man who founded the Methodist

Church. At twenty-two, the Oxford-educated Charles went with his brother John to America as a missionary. The Wesley siblings settled in Savannah, Georgia, where Charles preached to prosperous settlers and their slaves. His messages were largely ignored by the American establishment, who saw the young preacher as little more than an English peasant. Not only did those in Georgia not connect with the missionary, but he also failed to understand them. In 1738, having made more enemies than friends and converting no one, Charles Wesley returned home as a failure.

Back in London, Wesley began to work with George Whitefield, a dynamic speaker and evangelist who would be one of the leaders behind a growing antislavery movement. After his failure preaching to the upper class in America, Wesley shifted to preaching to those the Church of England largely ignored: the poorest of the poor. Like many of his day, Wesley composed original songs reflecting the theme found in that Sunday's message. Over the years, he wrote more than five hundred hymns, including "Christ the Lord Is Risen Today," "Love Divine, All Loves Excelling," and "Come, Thou Long Expected Jesus." Another, "Roll, Jordan, Roll," was written to illustrate a sermon on heaven. This song would not only enjoy popularity during Wesley's long life but also inspire a movement after his death.

Though people abducted from Africa and held in bondage were likely not on his mind when composing "Roll, Jordan, Roll," Wesley understood that almost all of God's children were a slave to something. Some were held captive by their vices, others by their jobs, a great number by poverty, and many to the cynicism that seemed to infect every facet of English life. He fully realized that those in his congregation needed a way to escape their bondage. Being a citizen of an island nation and living in a city where a river served as the transportation and economic hub, Wesley also understood how to employ the imagery of water to reinforce his message.

During the 1700s, water was both a highway and a boundary. It could take you where you wanted to go or keep you from the place you dreamed of living. Being baptized in water meant you walked out of that experience as a different person. Water washed away sins and provided a chance to begin a new life by leaving all the things that once held you back in the water. And when the crossing was complete, when you had left the old life behind, there was joy, grace, and acceptance.

The imagery of being a slave to this world and being freed by a trip over the Jordan was so strong that the song Wesley wrote to illustrate his sermon made a much greater impact than his message. When published, "Roll, Jordan, Roll" quickly became one of the most popular English anthems.

As with many English hymns, "Roll, Jordan, Roll" was imported to America. Some even believe that Wesley's friend and associate, George Whitefield, introduced it in the New World during one of his colonial crusades. Perhaps, because rivers were the principal form of transportation there, "Roll, Jordan, Roll" was first adopted by churches in Virginia and then taken across the South through camp meetings. These revival services were usually conducted in the open air and used no printed materials. Therefore, Wesley's "Roll, Jordan, Roll," as it was orally passed from community to community, experienced lyrical and melodic changes. In time, the arrangements used in these rural services produced a message and a tune much more American than British. It was also now less hymn than it was folk song. Because new music was constantly being introduced to Americans and few songbooks were distributed in the days before the American Revolution, "Roll, Jordan, Roll" might have been forever lost if it had not been adopted by a group of people the Wesley brothers and George Whitefield were intent on freeing: American slaves.

Much more than white Christians, black Americans saw "Roll, Jordan, Roll" as biographical. To them, God freeing the Israelites from bondage was not just ancient history; it was a rallying cry. The Jordan River had great spiritual significance to these newly converted African natives. They clung to the hope that if the Lord could free those ancient people, then surely he could provide a route to freedom for them. They adapted and changed Charles Wesley's hymn about heaven to suit their point of view. In its new form, the melody was infused with the beat and flavor of African folk music and the words rewritten to become less a story and more a prayer.

My brother you ought
To been there,
Yes, my Lord,
A sitting in the kingdom
To see Roll, Jordan, roll.

My mother, you ought
To been there,
Yes, my Lord,
A sitting in the kingdom
To see Roll, Jordan, roll.

Roll, Jordan, roll,
Roll, Jordan, roll.
I want to get to
Heaven when I die.

In the 1840s, with the growth of the abolitionist movement and the founding of the Underground Railroad as a method of smuggling southern refugees to freedom in the North, there finally seemed to be a route to freedom for American slaves. The key was navigating hundreds of miles of woods and fields and getting to the mighty Ohio River. On the other side was the promised land. And Charles Wesley's song about heaven suddenly took on a new role.

Initially, "Roll, Jordan, Roll" was sung in the fields as the slaves worked. But with the growth of the Underground Railroad, the Jordan became symbolic of the Ohio River, and the heavenly kingdom came to stand for any place a black man or woman could be free. And now, when "Roll, Jordan, Roll" was sung late in the night, it was a signal that a slave was making a break for the North and freedom. For those who beat the odds and heard the Ohio River roar, they would get to taste a bit of heaven on earth.

When the Civil War broke out, "Roll, Jordan, Roll" took on an even deeper and more urgent meaning. It morphed from a hymn into a battle cry for freedom. It was sung by white abolitionists at rallies and used in worship services in northern churches. It also became a part of political gatherings and was cited as one of President Abraham Lincoln's favorite songs. And on July 4, 1862, during a parade in Washington, DC, a group of hundreds of recently freed African American slaves marched and sang "Roll, Jordan, Roll" while accompanied by the cheers of thousands of spectators.

Today, like then, earthly slavery comes in many forms. People are held back by prejudice, poverty, war, destruction, disease, grief, and circumstance. Many become so beaten down that it is as if they are chained. Like the slaves, they are without hope and continually praying for relief. And like the early apostles, they are sustained during their long and trying days on earth by the promise of a heavenly release from pain.

For American slaves to gain freedom, free people had to build and run the Underground Railroad. Undertaking this effort posed a great risk. During the Civil War, millions sacrificed everything for souls they had never met. And simply because they sought to help the powerless, hundreds of thousands paid with their lives.

In Matthew 25:35–40, Jesus gave his followers a charge. They were to become like him by reaching out and touching the least of these. Today, when people consider Christ's challenge, they might want to think of the old hymn "Roll, Jordan, Roll." Through acts of sacrifice and grace, each Christian has a chance to guide a lost soul across treacherous water and to the peace that is waiting on the other side. The choice to go to heaven is ours, and the choice to guide others in that direction is ours as well.

To learn more about Charles Wesley, read John R. Tyson's *Assist Me to Proclaim: The Life and Hymns of Charles Wesley*, published by Eerdmans in 2008.

This Ole House

Stop collecting treasures for your own benefit on earth, where moth and rust eat them and where thieves break in and steal them. Instead, collect treasures for yourselves in heaven, where moth and rust don't eat them and where thieves don't break in and steal them. Where your treasure is, there your heart will be also.

Matthew 6:19–21

Many are judged by where they live. People drive by a house and automatically conjure up an image of the person who calls that place home. Therefore, it is hardly surprising that polls have found that one of the most common dreams is either building or buying a new home. In fact, one of the first things most people do when they win the lottery or get a large inheritance is buy a much nicer house. As has been said, "Appearances are everything"—although the Bible suggests something far different.

Christ taught that people should not worry about laying up treasures on earth. His lessons tried to get his followers to focus on doing the Lord's work in the here and now. He promised that by giving everything to serve others, they would be assured a heavenly home beyond their imagination. However, when faced with that challenge, most, like the rich young ruler, couldn't give up what they possessed and follow Christ. In a very real sense, in Jesus's time as now, what people owned or didn't own defined their security. It took an old house to get one man to fully grasp this lesson and to write it in a way that millions understood.

Stuart Hamblen was born in Texas in 1908. As a teen, this son of a Methodist preacher grew tired of the confining life of being a minister's kid and, much like the prodigal son, wandered across the West. Dressing like a cowboy, he embraced a life that mirrored his appearance. He was a gambler, fighter, and heavy drinker. In 1931, he arrived in Hollywood, where his ability to spin yarns landed him a gig on a radio program. Less than a year later, he met John Wayne and began acting. But his songwriting would earn him enough money to buy a nice home and a fancy car. His music also allowed him to finance the rowdy ways of his youth. By 1935, his arrest blotter for drunk and disorderly was so long that it took up several pages of a thick file folder.

Hamblen might have been a drunk, but his songwriting talent kept him from being homeless. The publishing royalties from hits such as "I Want to Be a Cowboy's Sweetheart" gave him security, but it was security without much hope. Each night of partying left him with a morning of misery. His hard life was exacting a huge toll.

In 1949, Hamblen was just forty-one but looked decades older. In one of his sober moments, he accepted an invitation to a tent revival led by an up-and-coming evangelist named Billy Graham. Immediately after that meeting, he gave up booze and began to study the Bible. Within months, he had taken his faith public via a radio program called *Cowboy Church of the Air*. Broadcast on Sunday mornings, this show featured the testimonies of many important show-business personalities and served as a forum for Hamblen to debut a new kind of music: Christian hymns cowboy style. For most of his radio audience, the best part of each show was hearing Hamblen tell the story behind his latest song. His new Christian-themed works, "Open Up Your Heart and Let the Sun Shine In," "The Lord Is Counting on You," "You Must Be Born Again," "Until Then," "Your First Day in Heaven," and "It Is No Secret," soon outsold many of his secular hits.

Though he no longer drank or gambled, Hamblen's old friends still loved to be around the gifted storyteller. So it was hardly surprising that John Wayne often asked the songwriter to go on hunting trips into the mountains. One of the things that often frustrated his hunting partners was Hamblen's curiosity. If he saw a cave, he had to explore it. If he spotted a field of flowers, he usually made a detour to smell them. And if he spied another hunter across a valley, he had to make the trek to meet him and find out his story. So in 1953, when Hamblen's party topped a ridge and spotted a small cabin a mile or so away, his buddies were hardly shocked that, even though it would mean a steep climb, Hamblen had to go check it out.

It took strenuous hiking to cover the distance, and the hunters were winded by the time they made it to within a hundred yards of the cabin. From a meadow, they could see that a few of the windows were cracked, the small porch drooped toward the north, and there were almost as many shingles scattered on the ground as affixed to the roof. Though the cabin looked deserted, Hamblen had to see what was behind those walls.

As the others watched, the songwriter made his way forward. When he approached the porch, he yelled out a greeting. His voice was answered by a dog's howl. Shocked, he hurried to the front door and knocked. The only reply was a few weak barks and continuous pawing at the entry. Confused, Hamblen turned and called for his friends to join him.

The hunters were faced with a dilemma. The door was locked, but the dog sounded frantic. They tried peering through the windows, but the cabin was too dark to see anything. Only the dog's now constant crying caused Hamblen and the others to put shoulders to the cabin's entry. When they pushed it open, they were greeted by a frail hound, his bones all but pushing through his skin. Looking past the dog, Hamblen spotted a bed. Strolling over, he noted a man who had likely died within the past week. On a nightstand were photos of what Hamblen guessed were family members. Around the small structure were a few dishes, a tablecloth, and some toys serving as reminders of a wife and children. The only other thing giving a clue as to who the man was and what he must have been thinking in the moments before his death was an open Bible. Hamblen picked up the well-worn book, and as he thumbed through the pages, he found notes written in the margins and verses underlined. It appeared the man must have known the words in the book very well. In silence, Hamblen glanced back to the body. For the first time, he saw a look of peace etched on the thin face and a slight smile on the lips. He might have died without another person around him, but he didn't seem to have been lonely or distressed.

After Hamblen said a short prayer, the hunting party walked outside to discuss their options. They were so deep into the mountains that they couldn't carry the body out, but they also couldn't just leave the man in his bed. On the porch, beside some boards, a can of nails, a saw, and a hammer, they found a shovel. Taking turns, they dug a grave behind the cabin. After the burial, one of the men looked at the poor state of the house and noted with a healthy degree of irony, "He's gone to a better place."

After he returned to Los Angeles, Hamblen couldn't wash the cabin scene from his mind. In an effort to pay tribute to a man who had died alone, the songwriter took up his pen and began to write what he assumed would be a sad ode to a lonely man's death. The story's theme was simple and centered on the poor state of the home. Because of the tools they found when searching for a shovel, it seemed logical that the owner was planning to fix up his shack, but sadly he died without completing the task. Still, the expression on his face indicated that death had come peacefully. So Hamblen guessed the old mountain man had not been worried about what he had left to do. In fact, he seemed ready to leave his work undone and move to a new location. And then, as if he was listening to Christ tell a parable, inspiration struck via a question. Why are people so worried about appearances that they forget about God's promise? With that in mind, it was time to write.

As he finished his new song, Hamblen realized what he had penned was much different from what he had intended. Rather than a mournful tale about a man dying alone and in poverty, the song had a decidedly hopeful perspective.

When Hamblen first sang "This Ole House" on his radio show, the station was flooded with calls asking where people could buy the record. One of those who fell in love with the musical story about leaving earth to go to a better home in heaven was the top female vocalist in the country: Rosemary Clooney. In 1954, she took "This Ole House" to number one on the pop music charts. The song that echoed Christ's warning of not measuring our lives by our possessions but by our service to others has been recorded hundreds of times in the past six decades.

Why is this song so remembered and beloved? Perhaps because it fully frames what is important and what is unimportant. For a Christian, the love experienced in life is ultimately far more fulfilling than the accumulation of riches, and the reward at the end of the journey on this earth really does mean we are moving to a better home. This old house is just temporary, but heaven is forever!

Farther Along

Faith is the reality of what we hope for, the proof of what we don't see.

Hebrews 11:1

Tempted and tried, we're oft made to wonder
Why it should be thus all the day long;
While there are others living about us,
Never molested, though in the wrong.

Refrain:
Farther along we'll know more about it,
Farther along we'll understand why;
Cheer up, my brother, live in the sunshine,
We'll understand it all by and by.

Sometimes I wonder why I must suffer,
Go in the rain, the cold, and the snow,
When there are many living in comfort,
Giving no heed to all I can do.

Tempted and tried, how often we question
Why we must suffer year after year,
Being accused by those of our loved ones,
E'en though we've walked in God's holy fear.

Often when death has taken our loved ones,
Leaving our home so lone and so drear,
Then do we wonder why others prosper,
Living so wicked year after year.

"Faithful till death," saith our loving Master;
Short is our time to labor and wait;
Then will our toiling seem to be nothing,
When we shall pass the heavenly gate.

Soon we will see our dear, loving Savior,
Hear the last trumpet sound through the sky;
Then we will meet those gone on before us,
Then we shall know and understand why.

In 2011 Shelby Seabaugh was one of the brightest young women ever to walk onto the campus of Ouachita Baptist University. A Christian studies major, she was five feet of energy who reflected in her speech, walk, and smile her faith and passion for life. Her thoughts were deep, her tone joyful, and her wonder childlike. With boundless energy and endless curiosity, coupled with incredible empathy and limitless patience, she reached out to those who were suffering or lost in an attempt to show them compassion, grace, and love. The blue-eyed brunette spent her summers as a counselor at a youth camp where scores of young kids hung on her every word and followed her every step. At just twenty-one, she was the ideal young woman whose future seemed unlimited. And then during a spring break, she died.

Shelby's father, Mike Seabaugh, was a pastor at a church in Magnolia, Arkansas. He had given his life to the Lord and with his warm smile and gentle wit had served as an inspiration to thousands. Yet when his daughter, who reflected all the values Mike embraced, died in her sleep, and when the autopsy revealed no cause for her passing, he had no answers, only questions. Why Shelby? Why was someone who had so much to give taken before she had the chance to realize her potential?

To many in their flock, preachers are the men with all the answers. They can find just the right words to comfort the sick, bring solace to a mourning family, or lead a doubting soul to Christ. What is so often forgotten when listening to the prayerful words that come from the mouths of pastors is that they are human too. They suffer the same pains, temptations, doubts, fears, and heartaches as do the members of their congregations.

When tragedy strikes good people, the question that almost always follows is, "How could God do this?" This question is so overwhelming that few preachers try to address it in sermons. When they are forced to offer words, the most common advice seems to be, "Someday you will understand."

More than a century ago, a small-town Missouri preacher faced heartache that seemed too much to bear. He and his wife had buried not just one child; over the course of several years, they had lost all six of their children to sudden illnesses. From an infant to a boy in his late teens, they were taken for seemingly no earthly reason. This series of losses was the capstone on a life of misery and suffering that few outside of Job had ever endured.

William Stevens was born in Missouri in 1862. His father, a Union soldier, was court-martialed and sentenced to a federal prison. Buel Stevens spent six months behind bars before he was found innocent of mutiny and released. It was later proven that the army had used the trumped-up charge to keep demoralized soldiers in line, but the stain of his time behind bars would haunt the man and his family for decades.

When Stevens's father was in prison, he lived with his uncle. Then the relative who had found the grace to take in the toddler suddenly died of a heart attack. Not long after this unexpected death, the uncle's seventeen-year-old son also passed away. It was as if Stevens's family was cursed.

By 1880, Stevens had married and surrendered to Christian service. After traveling across the country as evangelists, he and his wife established a church in Queen City, Missouri, where he adopted the life of a full-time pastor and she prepared for motherhood. The couple had six children, and all but one died before reaching their teens. A son, Waldo, lived until he was nineteen. Then on the verge of a life in an exciting new century, he passed away for no recognizable reason.

Perhaps because of Stevens's suffering, his church grew. People wanted to meet the man who had the conviction to trust God even after dealing with one unfathomable loss after another. As he bravely stood and preached the gospel each week, the community saw their minister as a shining example of unshakable faith. Yet hidden beneath a wall of resolve, Stevens was struggling to find reasons to live.

Though he didn't exhibit it, depression consumed much of Stevens's life. He was lost chasing questions that seemingly had no answers. In his prayers, he asked time and time again what he had done to deserve this burden and pain. And again and again he heard no response and was given no direction.

Bible study also failed to help Stevens resolve his issues. Though the words on the pages gave him material for sermons to lead others to Christ, they didn't answer the preacher's own haunting questions, and those questions were driving the man away from God. Whether he was in his office, with his wife in their lonely and mournful home, or walking down the street, *Why?* echoed inside his head. That three-letter word came to torment his waking hours and invade his sleep. He simply couldn't escape it. Every new view, each sound, and every glimpse of a child seemed to scream, *Why?*

Ironically, Stevens's tragedies made him not only an inspiration but also a target. Some pointed to the pastor's life as a way of justifying their lack of faith. They used the preacher's endless heartaches as proof that God didn't exist. Stevens even became the reason some saw no reason to live in the straight and narrow.

As he wrote in a sermon, one day when he was so frustrated and filled with grief that he could barely breathe, he escaped from his office to the sanctuary. As if being led, he bypassed the altar and moved to the organ. Sitting on the bench, he played around with the pedals and keys until he struck a chord and held it. Just hearing the series of notes linger in the air brought him an immediate sense of peace. He was so moved that he played this same chord over and over again. It was still echoing in the sanctuary when he finally rushed back to his office ready to address the question on the lips of millions: "Why me?"

That chord-inspired sermon was delivered and went nowhere. But rather than give up, Stevens opted to put his insights into a poem. As the lines fell into place, he began to realize he was writing his autobiography.

The first verse centered on the unfairness he saw in his life and the lives of others. Much like the first few lines of Longfellow's "I Heard the Bells on Christmas Day," the words Stevens scribbled renounced faith and pointed out that God was often not there for those who worshiped him and kept his commandments. The second verse repeated the cry of a man drowning in pain. On first read, the poem was more a suicide note than a tribute to a saving Lord. If he had quit writing after those first two stanzas, the preacher would have penned nothing more than the pitiful, hopeless cry of a man who had given up on life. But after wallowing through his darkness and grief, Stevens next penned words that embraced faith and hope.

As a preacher, he had spent years trying to give answers to those wrapped in pain. But after playing the chord on the organ, he had been awakened to the fact that he lived in an imperfect world. Jesus recognized that and spoke of it. How had he missed that even his Savior had experienced pain and anguish as a part of his life on earth? Thanks to humanity's fall from grace, life was not fair even for the faithful. Even the perfect Son of God had been crucified. Yet Jesus arose! That meant there was triumph over death, which confirmed that living for God had rewards. It also meant that given time, everything would be explained, and each question would be answered.

After setting his spiritual autobiography to music, Stevens shared it with his congregation. The response was so overwhelming that the preacher felt encouraged to seek a publisher for "Farther Along." Ironically, when it secured a place in a hymnal, the song written to help those going through great pain was all but ignored. Within twenty years, Stevens assumed he was the only one leaning on it during tough times. Then one day he turned on the radio—and heard the most famous gospel music group in the world singing his hymn. What was this?

In the midst of the Great Depression, the Stamps Quartet found the sheet music to "Farther Along" and felt its message was one that millions struggling in pain needed to hear. It proved to be such a popular concert number that it was reprinted in a hymnal by the Stamps-Baxter Music and Printing Company. Soon it was being sung by congregations across the country and continued to grow in popularity during World War II.

When people are going through difficult times, the most common phrase offered by Christians seems to be "This too shall pass." William Stevens surely heard those words countless times. Certainly, Mike Seabaugh did as well. But for most, those words fail to provide either help or hope. Stevens added to the thought "This too shall pass" by pointing out that in heaven, not only will we have a joyful life free from pain and loss, but we will also finally be given the answers as to why bad things happen to good people. It is said that patience is its own reward, and "Farther Along" assures us that the reward will be one that proves our faith was justified.

In the Sweet By and By

Heaven is declaring God's glory;
the sky is proclaiming his handiwork.

Psalm 19:1

There's a land that is fairer than day,
And by faith we can see it afar;
For the Father waits over the way
To prepare us a dwelling place there.

Refrain:
In the sweet by and by,
We shall meet on that beautiful shore;
In the sweet by and by,
We shall meet on that beautiful shore.

We shall sing on that beautiful shore
The melodious songs of the blessed;
And our spirits shall sorrow no more,
Not a sigh for the blessing of rest.

To our bountiful Father above,
We will offer our tribute of praise
For the glorious gift of His love
And the blessings that hallow our days.

*H*undreds of years ago, someone made a suggestion that has stood the test of time: you need to stop and look at the world around you. Many places in Psalms and Proverbs echo this suggestion. It is not too difficult to imagine that truth being worked into one of the parables of Christ. So why can't we shake out of our routines long enough to see the wonder around us? Why must we keep our heads down? Why don't we allow ourselves to have the faith to see beyond our troubles and problems and find that beautiful picture of grace that is there for us each day?

Imagine for a moment what it must have been like when early American settlers first saw the Rocky Mountains. Consider the emotions of the Native Americans as they looked down on the splendor of the Grand Canyon. Try to contemplate the wonders seen by Lewis and Clark. While some places today are as breathtaking as they were then, in many ways, we have not been very good stewards of this planet. Unlike when people first walked the earth, most of what we now see has been markedly changed by humans. Perhaps Paul's words about the clouded mirror found in 1 Corinthians are a reflection of how much God's perfect handiwork has been compromised by an imperfect world. Amazingly, it would take the ugliness humans inflicted on the earth to inspire one of the world's most popular hymns.

In 1866, a man who had seen God's unspoiled beauty at its most glorious and had also experienced human nature at its worst opened a drugstore in Elkhorn, Wisconsin. Sanford Fillmore Bennett was born in Eden, New York, in 1836, and like so many of that generation, his parents bought into the dream of being pioneers. When Bennett was two, the family moved west to Plainfield, Illinois. Bright, curious, and hardworking, Bennett enrolled at the Waukegan Academy at sixteen and within two years was teaching elementary students to read. He was still in his teens when he entered the University of Michigan. After completing his college work, he ended up in Elkhorn as the editor of the local newspaper. He provided the news for local citizens until he made the news by joining the Union Army. While in uniform, Bennett came to understand the horrors of war, the fragility of life, and the ugly nature of man.

Thanks to advances in weaponry, during the Civil War almost 700,000 died horrifically. In places that had once displayed some of God's most beautiful work, bodies littered crater-filled fields. In spots, the ground was so soaked with human blood that dirt became red mud. The scars of this war would forever change the earth and the people who walked it.

A much different Bennett returned to Elkhorn after the war. He looked and acted older, and his focus had changed.

After witnessing death and destruction on such a massive scale, writing for the local newspaper had lost its appeal. He was no longer interested in penning stories that revealed human shortcomings or frailty; instead, he was determined to find ways to heal hearts and lives. With this higher calling in mind, he bought a drugstore and began to study medicine.

His new business offered Bennett an opportunity to get to know almost all those living in and around Elkhorn. When they came into his store, the outgoing Bennett engaged his customers in conversation. Due to his gentle nature and warm smile, on cold winter days, many of his patrons would pull up a chair by the wood-burning stove to talk. Much as he had done when working for the newspaper, he asked questions that gave him insight into what was important and valued in each customer's life.

Joseph Webster was almost fifty when he first wandered into Bennett's drugstore. Webster was a local celebrity, a New Hampshire native whose brilliance had been identified as a child. His musical abilities were also astounding, and he had studied with composers such as Lowell Mason and George Webb. Upon completing his studies, Webster starred in stage shows and operas and, for a time, served as the pianist for the world-renowned Jenny Lind. A decade earlier he had composed the music for "Lorena," which had become the most popular song in the country before and during the Civil War. He was also the creative force behind "The Wildwood

Flower," a timeless tune that remained a recognized guitar standard a century and a half later.

After he retired from performing, Webster bought a saloon in Elkhorn and converted it into a respectable establishment that welcomed the town's most refined citizens. Though outwardly friendly, he never revealed too much of what was on his heart to anyone but Bennett.

On a cold winter day in 1867, Webster strolled into Bennett's drugstore and took a seat by the stove. He looked tired and haggard. His eyes were dark and his mood somber.

In the past, Bennett and Webster had talked about everything from politics to literature, but when Webster was melancholy, as he was on this day, the conversation usually centered on the ugliness of humanity. Bennett quickly discovered that on most days, Webster's depression was sparked by reminders of the war. On one day, his depression might be triggered by seeing a veteran missing a leg or an arm; on the next, it might be triggered by meeting a widow who was raising her children alone. In Webster's view, the war had robbed the earth of joy and optimism. How could a loving God allow things like this to happen?

Because of what he had seen firsthand, Bennett largely agreed with Webster's dour observations. During the war, many of his friends had died. And for what reason? America was still not united. There were still hard feelings on both sides. Even beyond the scars of war, life was brutal. Right in Elkhorn, scores of children became sick and slipped away before making it to school age. Their mothers never got over burying their children. So while he hadn't lost his faith in God, the destruction and death Bennett had witnessed first-hand made him question the nature of man.

As their morose conversation wore down, a weary Webster, after considering all the hopeless observations that had filled the last hour, sighed and said, "It will be better by and by."

Bennett considered his friend's statement. Would things ever really be better on earth? Would humans ever find a way to stop, listen, look at God's creation, and feel satisfied and blessed? Or would humans always be so consumed by their need to rule or possess that they would forever make the earth an ugly place? As he considered the dismal circumstances that had influenced his life, he turned his thoughts back to the kind, compassionate people who entered his store each day. He then thought about the beautiful scenes in the woods surrounding Elkhorn. Yes, the hope was there; you just had to stop long enough to see it. So while the sour Webster considered "by and by" to be a time when things were simply all right, Bennett turned the idea upside down to thoughts of "by and by" being the moment when things were perfect.

"What if it was a sweet by and by," the drugstore owner finally asked his friend. Then as the guest considered the observation, Bennett added, "That would make a good hymn."

Smiling for the first time since he entered the store, Webster replied, "Maybe it would."

As Webster sat silently, Bennett hurried to his desk and jotted down his thoughts. Within minutes, he had completed a poem and rushed the prose back to the sober saloon owner. Webster studied the words before picking up a pencil and scribbling down a few notes. He then asked to borrow Bennett's fiddle. As both men smiled, Webster played and Bennett sang "In the Sweet By and By." And suddenly, for at least two men, the world was a better and more hopeful place.

Thanks to Webster's contacts in the music business, "In the Sweet By and By" was quickly published. While the song brought immediate hope to two men awash in the ugly nature of humanity, it likely never would have become a part of the American landscape if not for the great revival movement that swept the United States in the last quarter of the eighteenth century. While thumbing through a new hymnal, Ira Sankey, one of the top vocalists of that era, discovered "In the Sweet By and By" and began singing it in front of the huge crowds that came to hear Dwight Moody preach. Thanks to this exposure, by the end of the decade, Bennett's words and Webster's tune were being performed in churches all over the globe.

The reason the fullness of God's creation is rarely seen is because humans have a way of ruining the view. Yet "in the sweet by and by," the pain, suffering, destruction, ugliness, and heartache will be gone, and our eyes will be opened to wonders we cannot begin to imagine. Death is therefore not a sentence but a release from imperfection.

Glory Train

Bless the God and Father of our Lord Jesus Christ! He has blessed us in Christ with every spiritual blessing that comes from heaven.

Ephesians 1:3

A common debate often centers on how people will get from earth to heaven. An African, captured and brought to America in the 1700s, envisioned that a ship, much like the one that had taken him across the Atlantic to slavery, would be the vehicle transporting him to a life filled with grace and freedom. He would later pen "The Old Gospel Ship," echoing his thoughts. Likely inspired by Christ's ascension, others wrote of literally flying with the angels to glory. The best known of these is "I'll Fly Away." For many, making that final journey would be much like transporting off the deck of the *Enterprise* from *Star Trek* fame and ending up materializing in heaven. Other songs such as "I'll Meet You in the Morning" portrayed the final trip being made during sleep. Believers would just go to bed and wake up in glory. Other popular gospel standards embraced a much more familiar method of crossing the Jordan. But one gospel song, first sung by a rock 'n' roll legend who was the inspiration for the term *teen idol* and written by a man whose childhood church was right beside a railroad track, focused on a train.

Trains played a vital role in the expansion of America. Without the invention of the "iron horse," the country's westward expansion would likely not have been so rapid. As more and more people booked tickets west, stories were written about everything from train robberies to wrecks to romantic meetings on the rails. And adults and children saw the powerful machines hauling passengers and freight as symbolic of the freedom, excitement, and romance that almost everyone wanted in their lives. While children dreamed of being engineers, adults saw riding a train as one of life's most fascinating adventures. A train could take them anywhere. It could transport them away from their troubles to a new life. It also offered what those suffering through heartache or hard times so desperately wanted: a ticket to a second chance.

For decades, taking a trip across the country by train was a leisurely and relaxed experience. By looking through the windows, people got to see places they had only read about and had an opportunity to study landscapes and cities in ways that provoked thought and conversation. And one of the most magical elements of each journey was dreaming about the destination at the end of the line.

During the golden age of the rails, preachers seized on the imagery found in train travel as inspiration for sermons. They painted verbal pictures of a trip that began with birth and wove stories of viewing one's life passing by. Listeners could envision their childhood, parenting years, and even old age as a trip. And after speaking of the various stops that a train made, the preachers usually ended their sermons with the train finishing its run and slowing at the station. The last question was almost always, "Where did your journey take you?"

No one knew more about the unexpected stops of life's train than Baker Knight. He was born in Birmingham, Alabama, on Independence Day in 1933. The Great Depression had plunged the Knights into poverty few could imagine, and in 1939, when Baker Knight's father died, things grew even worse. His mother turned the young boy over to relatives in order to give him a better chance at life. While this allowed Knight to have a roof over his head, things were still tough and often lonely.

Knight found inspiration at church. He fell in love with the lively gospel music that poured from the Stamps-Baxter hymnals. During the song service, he tapped his toes to the beat and sang at the top of his lungs. When the preacher began to speak, Knight often looked out the church's windows to watch the trains fly by. Those weekly daydreams of being onboard the locomotives likely fueled his passion for travel, and after graduating from high school, he joined the Air Force to see the world. During his two-year stint, he also embraced the other passion he had developed at church—music—and formed a band.

Upon his discharge, with guitar in hand, Knight boarded a train, returned to Birmingham, found a job in a factory, and at night began working in local clubs with a country music band. With an apartment and a car, the twenty-one-year-old felt as if he had the world by the string. After catching one of his performances and listening to songs Knight had written, a Music City talent scout suggested Knight go to Nashville. With no thoughts for a future and the promise of fame filling his head, Knight quit his job to pursue his passion. What seemed like a new beginning quickly looked more like a bitter end. After a few months of having his songs rejected, his car was repossessed, his pockets were empty, and meals were hard to come by.

The starving Knight prayed for a miracle, and when a friend told him about jobs as extras in Hollywood movies and television, it seemed his prayers were answered. Packing his guitar and the few clothes he owned, he headed west. A month later, with no job or prospects, a homesick Knight returned to a cheap apartment. For four weeks, he had attempted to land a job at stores, car lots, and restaurants. He had also spent a part of each day pitching his songs to publishers. No one wanted him or his music. Pulling an old jar off an otherwise empty shelf, he twisted the lid and poured his life savings onto a table. He counted the change three times. Each time the tally came up thirty-eight cents.

Now faced with a world in which he had no friends, nothing to eat, and no way to go home, Knight fell into a depression so deep there was no light. After saying a prayer, he toyed with the idea that perhaps death would be better than a life on the streets. And then came a knock on the door. On the other side was the second-hottest recording star in the world: Ricky Nelson.

A Nashville songwriter who had just made a trip to Los Angeles had told the teen idol about a man from Birmingham who had some good tunes. She had then informed Nelson that one of her friends had run into Knight pitching songs to a local publisher. A phone call later, the singer had the songwriter's address and headed over to meet the soon-to-be homeless man.

For a moment, Knight was filled with hope. Yet when Nelson listened to a few songs, nodded his head, thanked the songwriter, and left, Knight was crushed. He was about to head to a pawnshop to sell his guitar when there was another knock. This time it was a lawyer with a check and a contract. Ricky Nelson had been so impressed with Knight's tunes that he was offering a two-thousand-dollar advance if the songwriter would let the teen idol record and publish one of the songs he had heard him play. Within a few months,

"Lonesome Town," inspired by Knight's failures, topped the charts. It was the first of many hits Knight penned for Nelson.

About a year later, Nelson called Knight to talk about Elvis. Knight recalled their meeting this way:

> Ricky had really been impressed with the gospel music Elvis had recorded. He was already using a gospel quartet, the Jordanaires, on his sessions. He loved the music they sang, so he decided he wanted to cut some spiritual music too, and he didn't want to do anything traditional. He wanted me to write something original for him. I had a strong church background, so I thought about the songs I had grown up singing in church. When I took myself back in time to my musical roots, the spirit and inspiration came easily.[1]

A memory of the old train that passed by his childhood church set in motion Knight's writing. This time the train was going someplace far more important than Atlanta or Memphis; these tracks led to the promised land. The lyrics and music came easily and mirrored the romantic image that had long been associated with train travel. The words also embraced the excitement of knowing that heaven was the final stop and that, upon arrival, loved ones, including Knight's father, would be at the station to greet the passengers.

For a man who had once believed that death might be better than life, "Glory Train" was a testimony to the fact that prayers can be answered. When he had been at his lowest, when he had no friends and no future, a knock on the door changed his life. In fact, it brought a bit of heaven to earth.

After polishing his work, Knight took "Glory Train" to Nelson. A few weeks later, the singer assembled his team in the studio. Nelson's straightforward recording of "Glory Train" became the most unusual song in the teen idol's repertoire. This wasn't rock 'n' roll; this was pure gospel.

Knight figured his latest composition would be dropped into an album and forgotten, but that was hardly the case. Nelson opted to introduce "Glory Train" to a national television audience on *The Ozzie and Harriet Show*. Millions must have been shocked to hear a song that talked about Jesus, salvation, and heaven. Today, some cite this performance as the beginning of the contemporary Christian music movement aimed specifically at teens.

While many others might have painted a more vivid picture of heaven than did Knight, in "Glory Train," the songwriter captured all the elements of what a journey from this world to the next should mean to Christians. It is going to be exciting to board this train, the trip that follows will be filled with wonder, and the final destination is not one to be feared but anticipated. So many travelers get to their destination and find no one waiting, but in Knight's "Glory Train," loved ones will be at the station to greet them.

Ricky Nelson's "Glory Train" was filled with Baker Knight's own memories of his church experiences. Hymns inspired him to become a songwriter, and church experiences taught him the price needed to claim his spot in heaven. "Glory Train" doesn't pull punches; it clearly spells out that the only way to board the train is with a ticket and to claim Christ as the Savior who purchased that ticket. And that simple act makes all the difference in this world and the next!

To learn more about Baker Knight, read his *A Piece of the Big-Time (My Songs—My Success—My Struggle for Survival)*, published by AuthorHouse in 2005.

He Keeps Me Singing

Speak to each other with psalms, hymns, and spiritual songs;
sing and make music to the Lord in your hearts.

Ephesians 5:19

There's within my heart a melody;
Jesus whispers sweet and low,
"Fear not, I am with you, peace, be still,"
in all of life's ebb and flow.

Refrain:
Jesus, Jesus, Jesus,
sweetest name I know,
fills my every longing,
keeps me singing as I go.

All my life was wrecked by sin and strife,
discord filled my heart with pain,
Jesus swept across the broken strings,
stirred the slumbering chords again.

Though sometimes He leads through waters deep,
trials fall across the way;
though sometimes the path seems rough and steep,
see His footprints all the way.

Feasting on the riches of His grace,
resting 'neath His sheltering wing,
always looking on His smiling face,
that is why I shout and sing.

Soon He's coming back to welcome me
far beyond the starry sky;
I shall wing my flight to worlds unknown,
I shall reign with Him on high.

Everyone prays for a good road with no obstacles. Most dream of a world with few problems but great joy. Even so, very few can claim a life without challenges. Even for Christians, the path is not always easy. There are times when heartaches can't be avoided, moments when others needlessly inflict pain, and instances when disease and depression steal energy and enthusiasm. When hit with things that are unfair, many stagger and fall. Yet faith is not defined by our tragedies as much as by how we deal with them. That is when the true measure of faith is revealed. Luther Burgess Bridgers was tested like few could imagine.

As a pastor, Bridgers was often asked what he did when things were not going the way he planned. His responses were the same most Christians give: when the road was difficult, when storms set in, and when his stamina faded, he turned things over to God. Bridgers assured those seeking his counsel that he was confident that even in the darkest valleys, the Lord was beside him, and if he stumbled, Jesus would always be there to pick him up. He pointed out that suffering was not heaven-sent but because the world was imperfect. Then he almost always added that God's love was and would always be perfect. If people trusted in that, they wouldn't fall or fail. The advice was deeply spiritual, but would the man who gave it, the man who seemed to have such a blessed life, really follow it when times got tough?

Bridgers was born on February 14, 1884, in Margarettsville, North Carolina, into a family who had been serving God for generations. Not only was his father, James, a pastor, but in the early sixteenth century, his great-grandfather times eleven had been the rector of St. John the Evangelist Church in Gloucestershire, England. While his father taught the boy to respect all occupations and that all were vital in this world, the elder Bridgers emphasized that preaching was the highest of all callings.

While still a teen, Bridgers committed his life to Christian service and at eighteen left home to attend Asbury College in Wilmore, Kentucky. When asked why he chose Asbury over a host of schools that were far closer to his home, Bridgers explained that the Lord had guided him to the twelve-year-old Methodist school. He so strongly felt God's leading that he believed only at Asbury would he be given the tools he needed to live out his dream of leading souls to Christ.

As he started his education, Bridgers met who he felt was the most beautiful young woman in the world. Sarah "Sallie" Veatch, like Bridgers, was a dedicated Christian in search of a way to serve God. She was bright, outgoing, humble, and well-read. After a long courtship, Sallie and Bridgers married, convinced they were meant to work hand in hand. Until 1909, the husband and wife team served in a church in Perry, Florida. Then, inspired by the Methodist revival movement and the likes of Dwight Moody and Billy Sunday, Bridgers took a leap of faith. With his wife's full support, he resigned from the pulpit to become an itinerant evangelist. The couple knew this would be a difficult life. They understood it would sometimes mean long separations and no guaranteed income, but both Sallie and Bridgers also believed this was how God wanted them to serve.

Jumping onto trains, catching rides on stagecoaches, saddling up horses, and sometimes traveling by foot, Bridgers crisscrossed the southern United States sharing a message of salvation. While many evangelists of the time embraced the hellfire and brimstone method to persuade people to give up a sinful life, Bridgers preached of the joy found by walking with God. Within his messages, he painted heaven as being not a faraway destination but a place that could be previewed in life. He explained that a heart filled with faith couldn't help but be happy, so a man or a woman who loved the Lord tasted a bit of heaven each time they gave themselves to serving God's children. Bridgers's quick smile, wonderful laugh, and bright eyes reinforced his message. People swore that when they looked in his face, they could see a reflection of God's love and grace. And when Sallie and their sons accompanied the preacher on his journeys, their happiness also reflected the messages in Bridgers's sermons. This family loved Jesus and had complete faith in the Bible verses they so easily quoted.

Not only was Bridgers a gifted orator, but he also possessed a dynamic, rich voice. Like many preachers of his day, he often penned songs echoing the messages found in his sermons. Most of his compositions centered on the faith and happiness that could be found in devotion to God. And when the preacher sang his songs, almost everyone smiled.

Each night after services, people almost always asked the preacher this question: "Where does all your happiness come from?" Bridgers pointed to Scripture and the joy he found in his family. After months of answering in that way, he was inspired to pen a very personal song. The smiles he witnessed the first time he sang "He Keeps Me Singing" assured Bridgers that the message he lived was one that everyone wanted to believe and take to heart.

In the first verse and the chorus of his musical testimony, Bridgers outlined the reason he was preaching and why he had something to sing about. Unlike many earthly friends, Christ did not run and hide when things got tough. Jesus was there in both the good and the bad times. And Christ was not a historical figure but a constant companion. He didn't just live a long time ago; he still lived!

In the next verse, Bridgers admitted that his life was far from perfect. He made mistakes that brought pain. Yet during the moments when life seemed unfair, Jesus was there to carry him through. In other words, faith offered the power to take a broken life and make it whole.

The third verse talked about the leadership of Jesus. During challenging times when Bridgers was ready to turn back and give up, he noted footprints belonging to his Savior. Jesus had walked this path before him and had suffered just as men and women had suffered and still do. So to follow Christ in times of pain meant going to a place where perfection was realized and suffering would end.

The last two verses revealed the promise the preacher wanted so badly for others to see and accept. With Jesus at the center of their lives, they were safe and protected, and best of all, there was an incredible reward waiting. When Christians winged their way to glory, they would be surrounded by the loved ones they so dearly missed on earth. Therefore, funerals were a cause for celebration, not sadness.

The final message, all but hidden in the last verse, was the power gained in following Jesus. Those who listened to Bridgers were usually poor and powerless, but his song assured them that they would have a place beside the King of Kings. For a person whose possessions were few and who had little control over the things in life, that was something to look forward to and sing about!

Just a few months after Bridgers premiered his musical testimony, one of the greatest hymn writers in the world heard "He Keeps Me Singing." Charles Tillman was so moved by the new song that he bought the publishing rights and released this ode to joy in *The Revival #6*. Within a year, Bridgers's personal testimony quickly took its place as one of the most popular new hymns of the revival movement.

About a year after composing "He Keeps Me Singing," Bridgers was asked to lead a series of services several hundred miles from his home. His wife and three sons, who often traveled with the evangelist, decided this would be a good time to visit family in Harrodsburg, Kentucky. After taking his family to his in-laws, Bridgers climbed into a wagon to begin his trek to the meetings. As he looked back, he saw his wife standing by her father's front gate, a baby in her arms and two boys by her side. They were all blowing kisses. The remainder of his life he would talk about how that simple scene so deeply blessed him.

During the next two weeks, Bridgers often told stories about his family. In a variety of ways, some serious and some filled with humor, he described the joys of marriage and parenthood. And each night when the meetings wound down, the crowds would also blend their voices in "He Keeps Me Singing."

On March 26, 1911, a smiling Bridgers finished his final service and returned to his hotel. After packing his suitcase, he lay down to get a few hours of sleep. As he went to bed, he was overjoyed by thoughts of seeing his family again. Hours later there was a knock on the door. Roused from a deep slumber, Bridgers was informed there was a call for him in the lobby. After slipping on a robe, the preacher made his way down the hall and to the phone. The news was grim. A few hours earlier, at the very moment Bridgers was encouraging those at the revival to immerse themselves in the joy of a Christ-filled life, a fire had broken out in his in-laws' home. The flames were so intense that his wife and children could not escape.

For a few seconds, as he considered all he had lost, the preacher remained deathly silent. Then as the few gathered in the hotel lobby watched, he dropped to one knee and whispered, "Lord, I have preached the gospel to other people and told them it would comfort them in every hour of sorrow. Grant that this same gospel may comfort me."

A few days later, in a church where four coffins rested near the altar, Bridgers stood and led the congregation in "He Keeps Me Singing." Those in attendance were stunned to see Bridgers smile as he loudly sang, "I shall wing my flight to worlds unknown, I shall reign with Him on high." To those in the sanctuary, it was obvious that the grieving man's faith remained strong. More importantly, he seemed completely assured that his family was in a place where Christ's love had removed every bit of darkness and pain.

Bridgers immediately went back to his calling and continued to travel across the United States leading revivals. During

World War I, he did mission work throughout Europe and into Russia. Never once did anyone hear him question why his family had died. And when he did share the story of his wife's and sons' deaths, he followed it by leading those around him in "He Keeps Me Singing."

Faith goes beyond understanding; a strong faith endures even when hearts are shattered and things can't be explained. Faith has this ability because the Christian knows, as Bridgers did, that there will come a time when all of us will wing our flight to worlds unknown and once more be united with God in perfect love. That is something that should keep everyone singing!

Beyond the Sunset

Then the eyes of the blind will be opened,
and the ears of the deaf will be cleared.

Isaiah 35:5

Perhaps no man's gravestone is as appropriate as that of Virgil P. Brock. The majestic granite monument anchored in the soil of Oakwood Cemetery in Warsaw, Indiana, fully defines Brock's insight, talent, faith, and optimism. It is haunting knowing that the words of the song etched into that marker were not written during the composer's best days but rather when his faith was at its lowest ebb. And the most remarkable element of the story is that the man who showed him the light couldn't see it.

In 1936, Brock, who had been in the ministry since his teens, was one of those wondering if the American way of life was doomed. Like a great boxer facing weak opponents, the Great Depression was inflicting pain and

111

misery such as the world had rarely seen. Thanks to this economic chaos, once stable farm families had become migrants and successful entrepreneurs had lost their businesses and homes. While hope was in short supply, heartache was everywhere.

Now in their fifties, Brock and his wife, Blanche, were such gifted songwriters that even in the midst of economic hard times, their music sales generated enough revenue to maintain a middle-class living. Using the state of Indiana as a base, the pair traveled the singing school and convention circuit, teaching tens of thousands the nuances of shaped-note arrangements and harmonies. During these tours, Brock was struck by the sheer hopelessness he saw in the eyes of those he was instructing. Mournful people were singing about faith while struggling with losing their own.

Brock often sat down and visited with those who had come to listen to the composer sing optimistic offerings such as "Sing and Smile and Pray" and "Let God Have His Way." While most of these fans praised Brock's ability to write such uplifting words, many admitted they saw no light in their own lives. They explained that the Depression had left them uprooted and lost. As he looked into the faces of men and women he had known for several years, Brock noted that worry had aged them decades in just a couple of years. Worse yet, hunger ate at their stomachs and doubt chewed on their souls. Many were fighting the darkness, which appeared to be winning. Simply put, they had no hope.

"Will things ever get better?" was the one question Brock was asked over and over again. Coming from a man who always sported a smile on his face and a spring in his step, his assurances that God was with them seemed to ring hollow. And so when he couldn't find the words to give them hope, when quoting Scripture did not help, and when his songs fell flat, he turned to the actions of a president and encouraged men and women that programs such as the WPA and the CCC were just the beginning of things turning around. Still, in an era when one-time millionaires sold apples on New York street corners and once proud farmers were picking fruit a thousand miles from the place they had called home, the darkness seemed much stronger than the light. In time, even the optimistic Brock began to feel the weight of American's depression. Soon it became harder and harder for him to preach and sing about faith to people who had lost everything.

As he tried to mask his own doubts with a smile, Brock sensed he desperately needed relief from the hopelessness confronting him at concerts and conventions. So for the first time in decades, he took a break and stepped away from the gospel music circuit. When he noticed Brock's anguish, music publisher Homer Rodeheaver invited the songwriter to Winona Lake, Indiana, to spend some time at the businessman's retreat. At the urging of Blanche, Brock accepted.

Within hours of arriving, Brock experienced a peace he hadn't felt in years. Over the next few days, he walked the trails, fished, enjoyed the company of his wife, reflected on his faith, read the Bible, and observed nature, but more importantly, he also pretended the problems of the world didn't exist. For a few days, there was no poverty, despair, or angst—at least none he could see.

During his stay at Winona Lake, Brock's cousin and his wife came to check on him and Blanche. Horace Burr had a special relationship with Brock. They were more like brothers than cousins. And Burr, who had been blind since birth, offered a perspective that was far different from what the composer could find anywhere else. As Brock guided Burr along paths or they sat by the lake, the two spoke of both hope and hopelessness. And it was Burr, a man who had spent his life in the darkness, who kept emphasizing that trials were just temporary and there were better days coming. He assured the songwriter that he could see them. Brock likely felt that if his blind cousin could actually look into the faces of the men and women the composer had met, he would not be so optimistic. In this case, maybe blindness was a gift.

After supper one evening, Brock and Blanche, along with Burr and his wife, retired to a porch on the side of the retreat. There was no wind, and the summer's heat was now disappearing. As Brock eased into a deck chair, the sun seemed to meet the placid lake, and across the water, a thousand shades of orange, red, and blue mixed together on a canvas only nature could create. As Brock took in a splendor that even the newly developed Technicolor cameras couldn't have fully captured, he became mesmerized. He likely would have remained mute, lost in wonder until the sun slipped into the lake, if his cousin hadn't remarked, "A storm is building."

The blind man's keen hearing had evidently picked up rolling thunder that was too faint for the others to hear. Moving his gaze to the left, Brock noted a thunderhead now reflecting the setting sun's glow. Like the lake, the cloud was ablaze with vibrant color, and from time to time, a burst of lightning displayed the power coming their way.

As the two opposing forces of nature rushed to meet each other, the sun vowing to hang on to every second of the day and the storm determined to cast the world into darkness, Burr commented, "That's the most beautiful sunset I've ever seen."

The shocking observation caused Brock to move his eyes from the lake to the man sitting a few feet away. How could the blind man make such an observation? He had seen none of nature's glory; he had not witnessed the myriad colors or the moment when the sun had met the lake's clear waters.

Burr must have sensed Brock's shock because he softly added, "Oh, I can see. It may be through others' words, but I can see the sunset. Better yet, I can see beyond it."

Over the course of the next few minutes, the storm grew closer. As lightning lit up the heavens and thunder shook the home, the completely relaxed Burr seemed to be looking right into the clouds. In the moments when the storm grew

115

wild and wicked, the blind man showed no fear but instead seemed confident that in time the storm would pass. The next day the sun would be back and would again set over the lake.

Pulling Blanche to one side, Brock whispered to her about his cousin being able to see what he had missed. He had never really thought beyond the sunset. He had just assumed that all that was there was night. But when the sun set on a life and the storms disappeared, there would be a world beyond filled with glory, wonder, and hope.

Blanche smiled and nodded before suggesting they go inside to pray and then write. And with the image of the sunset set against the coming storm, the Brocks constructed a song with four sides. Essentially, it was a square, and each wall of that square embraced a different theme.

The first verse centered on the world as it was at that moment. The lyrics told the story of life framed against dynamics of the Great Depression. The message was that the world was not fair. Sometimes people worked hard and still had nothing to show for it. While this was a verse meant to provide hope for those suffering under horrific economic conditions, the Brocks had unknowingly also put forth a lifeline for those dealing with sickness and death. The ultimate lesson of the opening stanza was that darkness and pain were temporary and a new dawn was coming.

In the second verse, Brock drew on Burr's observation about the thunderstorm. It would soon pass, and when it did, everything would be fine. So beyond the storm and the sunset, as people gathered in heaven, there would be no unexpected trouble to fear. On top of that, grief and darkness would be unknown.

In the third verse, the couple examined the darkness that came after the sunset. In a world of unknowns, how could people find their way? The answer was that God's hand was there to guide them. On top of that, in life, Jesus was with those who had been treated unfairly. He lifted the weak and insecure, he touched those others avoided, and he was still there for those who struggled through a modern world. Best of all, if people had faith in him and kept on the straight and narrow, Jesus would guide them to a place where trials ended in victory. Though written for those living through the Great Depression, this message was universal. In a very real sense, it was Scripture brought to life in a new format but with the same message of faith and hope.

The final verse was likely inspired by the singing conventions the Brocks attended. Year after year, they went back to the same places and renewed old friendships. These joyful events were as much about bonds being restored as they were about worship. This stanza promised a time when everyone would celebrate together again. This assurance of families gathered around the table and of stories being shared was one of the most powerful messages ever crafted into a hymn.

When a song is penned at a music publisher's home, it doesn't take long for it to get into print. In less than six months, "Beyond the Sunset" was being sung at revivals and in churches. In less than five years, the song inspired by the sight of a blind man became one of the nation's most beloved and well-known hymns.

Brock's struggle to comfort those caught in the Great Depression pushed him into personal depression. For a while, he became lost and blind to the hope found in walking with Jesus. Then his cousin, who had never viewed any of God's wonders, taught Brock how to see beyond the sunset. In that moment, Brock realized he had to see God's promise of heaven in order to offer hope and comfort to those lost in darkness on earth.

Virgil Brock died at the age of ninety-one, and inscribed on his tombstone are all 111 words of his most famous composition. Writing "Beyond the Sunset" restored Brock's faith and optimism, and its message has remained a beacon of hope during dark days for millions of others too.

Swing Low, Sweet Chariot

Then you will know the truth, and the truth will set you free.

John 8:32

Refrain:
Swing low, sweet chariot,
Comin' for to carry me home.
Swing low, sweet chariot,
Comin' for to carry me home.
Well, now they're comin' for to carry me home.

Well, now I looked over Jordan and what did I see
Comin' for to carry me home.
There was a band of angels a comin' after me
Comin' for to carry me home.

Well, I'm sometimes up and I'm sometimes down
Comin' for to carry me home.

But I know my soul is heavenly bound
Comin' for to carry me home.

Well, now if you get there before I do
Comin' for to carry me home.
Tell all of my friends that I'm a comin' too
Comin' for to carry me home.

*W*hether you are a child or an adult, one of the most fascinating stories found in the Old Testament is that of Ezekiel and the chariot. Even though it happened a few thousand years ago—when a prophet looked up and spied a shiny, sparkling vehicle, driven by angels, that spit fire and descended from heaven to earth—the events of that day still make an impact. It is one of those wow moments in history. And while "Swing Low, Sweet Chariot" may not draw its message from Ezekiel, the image of the prophet and the chariot had to be on the songwriter's mind.

As I watched, suddenly a driving storm came out of the north, a great cloud flashing fire, with brightness all around. At its center, in the middle of the fire, there was something like gleaming amber. And inside that were forms of four living creatures. This was what they looked like: Each had the form of a human being, though each had four faces and four wings. Their feet looked like proper feet, but the soles of their feet were like calves' hooves, and they shone like burnished bronze. Human hands were under their wings on all four sides. All four creatures had faces and wings, and their wings touched each other's wings. When they moved, they each went straight ahead without turning. As for the form of their faces: each of the four had a human face, with a lion's face on the right and a bull's face on the left, and also an eagle's face. The pairs of wings that stretched out overhead touched each other, while the other pairs covered their bodies. Each moved straight ahead wherever the wind propelled them; they moved without turning. Regarding the creatures' forms: they looked like blazing coals, like torches. Fire darted about between the creatures and illuminated them, and lightning flashed from the fire. The creatures looked like lightning streaking back and forth.

As I looked at the creatures, suddenly there was a wheel on the earth corresponding to all four faces of the creatures. The appearance and composition of the wheels were like sparkling topaz. There was one shape for all four of them, as if one wheel were inside another. When they moved in any of the four directions, they moved without swerving. Their rims were tall and terrifying, because all four of them were filled with eyes all around. When the creatures moved, the wheels moved next to them. Whenever the creatures rose above the earth, the wheels also rose up. Wherever the wind would appear to go, the wind would make them go there too. The wheels rose up beside them, because the spirit of the creatures was in the wheels. When they moved, the wheels moved; when they stood still, the wheels stood still; and when they rose above the earth, the wheels rose up along with them, because the spirit of the creatures was in the wheels.

The shape above the heads of the creatures was a dome; it was like glittering ice stretched out over their heads. Just below the dome, their outstretched wings touched each other. They each also had two wings to cover their bodies. Then I heard the sound of their wings when they moved forward. It was like the sound of mighty waters, like the sound of the Almighty, like the sound of tumult or the sound of an army camp. When they stood still, their wings came to rest. Then there was a sound from above the dome over their heads. They stood still, and their wings came to rest.

Ezekiel 1:4–25

If we had been in Ezekiel's shoes, if we had witnessed what he saw that day, most of us likely would not have thought the powerful, fire-belching machine was a chariot. In our stories, it probably would have been an airplane or a spaceship. But when put into the context of the time, Ezekiel's description makes perfect sense. In the Old Testament, the fastest and most impressive form of transportation was the chariot. It was used by generals, high officials of government, and royalty. And to put the use of this concept into even sharper focus, we must remember that the common man rarely got to touch a chariot much less ride in one.

Earlier in the Bible, another scriptural giant, Elijah, spotted a flying chariot. Once again, the vehicle came from heaven, but rather than just make an appearance, it landed and took Elijah back to his home with God. Thus, that chariot earned a spot in transportation history that few others can claim as it made a nonstop trip from this life to the next.

> They were walking along, talking, when suddenly a fiery
> chariot and fiery horses appeared and separated the two of
> them. Then Elijah went to heaven in a windstorm. Elisha
> was watching, and he cried out, "Oh, my father, my father!
> Israel's chariots and its riders!" When he could no longer see
> him, Elisha took hold of his clothes and ripped them in two.
>
> 2 Kings 2:11–12

With this kind of imagery and an eyewitness account of a
final trip to heaven being made using a horse-drawn vehicle,
it is little wonder that people began to think of the chariot
as the conveyance that connects this life to the next. Putting
this concept into a song that would bring the full meaning
of that trip to life would take a man whose value was once
measured by the dollars he brought on an auction block.

In legal terms, Wallace Willis was considered three-fifths
of a human being. At least that is the way the United States
Census Bureau saw the African American slave who was
owned by a Choctaw Indian. While prejudice initially united
the owner and the slave, it also drove them out of the South
and into the Oklahoma Territory. In 1840, white government
officials decided that the man who owned Willis could not
legally own land in Alabama. As a Choctaw, he did not have
that right. With little warning, the Native American was
stripped of his possessions and kicked off his farm. He and
his slave were then escorted to the Indian Territory and given
orders never to return to the South.

Though the move was frightening, Willis found two remarkable things in his new home. The first was freedom. No longer did someone own him or his wife. The second was acceptance. The Native Americans who lived in that area, most of whom were also refugees from the Deep South, didn't judge people by the color of their skin but rather by the character of their heart. Thus, the former slave was seen as an equal.

Willis impressed his new neighbors with his intelligence, creativity, hard work, and honesty. His character and generous actions also paved the way for his new friends to note that Willis was a deeply committed Christian. Willis shared his faith as easily as he shared his table. More importantly, he lived his faith through his passion for helping the poor and displaced. He and his wife fed those who were hungry and took care of orphaned children. Yet Willis didn't see acts of charity as enough. He believed he needed to spiritually grow to become an even better neighbor, friend, and mentor.

To further his understanding of the God whom he believed had saved him, the former slave learned how to read. He spent his spare hours sitting outside his home or by the fireplace studying the Bible. The stories of Ezekiel seeing the chariot and Elijah's trip to heaven so fascinated him that he read them again and again. He also shared these biblical adventures with friends. Sensing that music might be a better way to open young minds to the Bible, Willis opted to compose a song for the children at a local Indian school.

124

As he wrote, there can be little doubt that Willis was influenced by his own life experiences, and many of them mirrored what he read in the Bible. Like so many, he was a refugee who had been abused by powerful people. Like Moses, he had been a slave who was now free. Like the children of Israel, he was living in a foreign land.

Not far from his house, the Red River separated the Indian Territory from Texas. During the spring floods, the Red was a raging stream almost impossible to cross. Men had died trying. So in the former slave's mind, getting from this world to the next must be like crossing a dangerous and powerful river. While you could see a better life on the far bank, getting to it required a miracle. And in this case, the miracle was born of faith and came in the form of a chariot like the one that had picked up Elijah. With all of these thoughts and experiences in his mind, he went to work.

Willis's "Swing Low, Sweet Chariot" had the African feel of songs sung by slaves in the fields of the South. Like those of the spirituals, the lyrics were straightforward and the tune deliberate. The song's story was both biographical and universal in that it reflected the experiences and emotions of those who worked hard and received little. For these desperate people, time dragged by and the only thing providing any comfort or hope was what they could almost see but were not allowed to have: freedom. To most slaves, only God could give that gift.

Willis taught his song to the children at Old Spencer Academy, and it likely never would have escaped the Oklahoma hills if not for a visitor to the area. Alexander Reid had been given the task of teaching Native American children and heard Willis teaching "Swing Low, Sweet Chariot" to some new students. Reid was so impressed with the song that he transcribed the lyrics and melody and mailed them to the director of Fisk College in Nashville, Tennessee. The Jubilee Singers, the school's black gospel choir, performed Willis's spiritual during a national tour. It proved so popular that "Swing Low, Sweet Chariot" was published. Within a decade, the song's popularity had spread so far that an English queen declared it her favorite American spiritual and a resident of the White House asked for an encore.

"Swing Low, Sweet Chariot" has now been recorded hundreds of times and is the best-known of all the pre–Civil War spirituals. It is also one of the few Negro spirituals that can be traced to its composer.

While inspired by two stories found in the Old Testament, "Swing Low, Sweet Chariot" has a New Testament message. In reality, it is a testimony of the rewards that come from a life well lived coupled to the promise of a reunion with loved ones in a place where everyone is equal and free. And the fact that God is sending a chariot for all those who have accepted Christ means that, thanks to grace, a slave gets to ride in a vehicle that on earth was reserved for only those of social standing or political power. So few images define love, grace, equality, and acceptance better than this musical snapshot from Bible history.

Child of the King

You are all God's children through faith in Christ Jesus.

Galatians 3:26

*I*n 1918, a world war was winding down, and for the first time, the United States was flexing enough military and industrial muscle to be ranked as one of the world's greatest powers. America was now producing the products those all around the globe wanted and reshaping the globe's views of literature and entertainment. With the spotlight firmly fixed on North America, immigration to the United States was skyrocketing. Millions believed the only way to succeed and find happiness was to leave the Old World and make a life in a new one. To them, the United States was the place where dreams could be realized. They left all they knew to journey to a home with little more than faith and hope.

On a hot summer day in 1918, not far from Mexia, Texas, a child was born to a cotton broker and a piano teacher. The young couple named their daughter Cindy, and while the Walkers had their share of hopes and dreams, unlike millions fleeing a war-scarred Europe, they believed that everything they wanted and their daughter needed could be found without leaving home.

By the time she could walk, Cindy Walker was singing, and long before she started school, she was performing in her grandfather's church. This blonde bundle of energy was so entranced with music that she would sing in a living room, in a school, or on a street corner. She would later say that she was born looking for a stage, and if someone asked to hear Walker perform, she was always ready.

What amazed most adults was not the grown-up voice coming out of the tiny child's body; it was her ability to compose music. Perhaps this talent was a part of her DNA. Her grandfather, F. L. Eiland, had written several well-known hymns, including "Hold to God's Unchanging Hand," and the child had witnessed scores of people travel hundreds of miles just to talk about his music. Eiland encouraged his granddaughter to sing what was written on her heart, not what she found in songbooks. With the older man's advice ringing in her head, Walker went to work. By her teens, she had penned more than a hundred songs and was introducing them on her own local radio show. As happy as she was to perform, she was also frustrated. Her small hometown

128

was both a blessing and a curse. It gave her a platform but limited her exposure. Just like the refugees fleeing Europe, she was determined to find a way to escape the limits of her life and chase her dreams.

At the same time Cindy Walker was trying to find a way to escape her hometown, the Great Depression was crushing millions. And while the Walkers were secure, they fully recognized how bleak things were for their friends and neighbors. In a world so unstable, their goals for their daughter centered on keeping her close and safe. Their prayers were not of stardom but of Walker finding a husband who could provide a comfortable living and a secure future deeply rooted in Texas dirt.

Walker had a different vision, and a great deal of that came from a life grounded in church and faith. She saw her talent as God given and felt it would be a sin not to use it. So rather than hide her light under a basket, she constantly searched for ways to share it. Even in the face of a number of closed doors, she refused to give up. She wrote letters to publishers and entertainers and went out of her way to meet anyone with connections to the entertainment industry. At age twenty-one, when she accompanied her parents on a trip to the West Coast, she set caution to the wind. While her parents were using this business trip as an excuse to see Hollywood, Walker packed her guitar with plans to stay in the entertainment capital forever.

During their first days in California, her parents were fully embracing the role of tourists and seeing the sights. Walker

was looking too, but not at the Hollywoodland sign or the famous theaters, and when they drove down Sunset Boulevard,
she spied what she wanted. With a loud voice, she demanded
her father stop the car. When he asked why, she announced
she was going to wrangle her way into Bing Crosby's office
and sing one of her songs. The elder Walker told his daughter
she was crazy. She smiled, admitted that he might be right,
but said it was time to take a step of faith. After all, God was
giving her a chance to chase a dream, and it would be a sin
not to use it. What excited the daughter frightened the father.
What would happen when she was rejected? He figured that
losing her dream just might destroy her. Try as he could, he
failed to dissuade her. So rather than extend an argument that
had gone on for several minutes, he found a parking place,
sadly watched Walker exit the car, and deeply sighed as she
raced down the block.

As the Walkers waited, their daughter walked into Bing
Crosby Enterprises, bluffed her way past the receptionist,
and knocked on the door of Bing Crosby's brother. Upon
finding out the pretty, talkative woman was from Texas and
knowing Bing was looking for a cowboy song for his next
recording session, Larry politely listened as she sang "Lone
Star Trail." A few phone calls later, Walker found herself
headed to Paramount Studios, where Bing Crosby was working on a movie. On the set, she picked up her guitar and
confidently sang her song to one of the most popular entertainers in the world. The crooner was immediately impressed

and asked to hear a few more of her compositions. Sensing her potential, Crosby suggested the Walkers extend their stay in California. Within a few days, the young woman from Texas had a recording contract, was taking publicity photos, and was watching as Crosby cut "Lone Star Trail."

Within a year, Walker established herself as the queen of the western songwriters. In an era when cowboy movies ruled the box office, Walker wrote scores of hits. By 1944 she was penning twenty songs a week, and that didn't meet the demands for her tunes. By the end of the decade, more than fifty artists representing every major musical genre had recorded at least one of her songs. Thanks to her success, everyone in the entertainment business knew and respected her. She was constantly invited to the big parties, was interviewed by the press, appeared in movies, and was a regular guest on radio shows. And the woman from a small Texas town could claim that her closest friends were the most famous people in the world. And yet with fame, fortune, and more awards than she had wall space, Walker was lost in the spotlight. There was something missing. Even with all her accomplishments, the queen of the songwriters found herself longing for the place she had always wanted to leave, the place that had not been big enough for her dreams: home.

Shocking the entertainment establishment, Walker packed her belongings and moved back to Mexia, Texas, to live with her widowed mother. Once in central Texas, she put her awards in boxes, hid them under her bed, and slipped into a routine of joining clubs, going to church, and doing her own shopping. Along with the pop music she was still churning out, she dipped back into a musical style that reflected the values she had been taught as a child and had maintained even while living in Hollywood. The lyrics in these new works reflected not just the grace found in living a life of faith but also the promise of a world beyond this one in which peace, hope, love, and compassion would be realized.

As she scribbled notes, she found herself dwelling on two things. The first was that she was the child of really good parents. Walker's mom and dad had not just loved her; they had sacrificed for her. Even though they had not wanted her to embrace a life away from home, they had paved the way for her to realize her dreams and use her talent. Being their daughter had been one of her greatest blessings. Second, more than just the daughter of a cotton broker and a piano teacher, she was also a child of God. And the hope found in that thought was the message she had to share. With a portfolio that already included hits such as "Cherokee Maiden," "Dusty Skies," "Silver Spurs," "Oklahoma Hills," "Sugar Moon," "China Doll," "Dream Baby," "In the Misty Moonlight," and "Distant Drums," Walker set to work writing a song that looked at this world and beyond it. It would be her testimony and a composition that talked about the joy of going home.

The message found in "Child of the King" shows that Walker believed that as a child of royalty, she had to hold herself to a higher standard. And the reward for doing so was getting to live the ultimate dream: to sing in heaven. For a woman who had everything, that meant more than anything.

One of Walker's biggest hits was the classic ballad "You Don't Know Me." The song tells the story of a woman who was in love with someone who walked past her each day without even knowing she existed. While "You Don't Know Me" was musical magic, in Walker's "Child of the King," she assured everyone that God knew them and cared about them and that there was a home they could return to where a father was waiting to greet his children.

We are all pilgrims while on earth. We search for ways to make our dreams come true, but the fact is that those who know Christ also realize that home is not where the heart is but rather where the soul resides. Heaven is more than a dream or a destination; it is a welcoming home, and life is the highway that takes us there.

A bestselling book once asked if a person could happily return to the place where they were born, and since its release eighty years ago, *You Can't Go Home Again* has sparked a debate on that very question. Cindy Walker's life seems to provide the answer. When she died in 2006 and made her last move, there can be little doubt that she was thrilled to be home.

Peace in the Valley

"Allow the children to come to me," Jesus said. "Don't forbid them, because the kingdom of heaven belongs to people like these children."

Matthew 19:14

I am at peace with my decision."

Consider for a moment what that means. A person who can make that declaration has likely studied each angle and carefully thought through every ramification. And for many, they have also trusted God to take over what they can't control. Surprisingly, for the man who gave the world one of gospel music's greatest songs, trusting God and finding peace did not come easily.

Thomas A. Dorsey left a legacy of music composition so rich that he has justifiably been called "the father of gospel music." He was born among former slaves in Georgia in 1899. His father was a preacher, and his mother was an organist. Services took place every night of the week, so he was literally raised in church. In elementary school, he learned to play the piano. Though he knew well the music he heard in his father's sanctuary, thanks to family trips to Atlanta, he was drawn to the jazz sounds coming from gin joints. By the time he was a late teen, his love affair with blues had lured him to Chicago, where he made a living playing ivory keys in night clubs. In the good times and relaxed living of the Jazz Age, when illegal booze flowed and the nation was awash in money, the young man's talents were easy to market. By twenty-one, now completely immersed in a world that emphasized secular pleasure, Dorsey was writing original music and had landed a gig as the pianist for the popular jazz vocalist Ma Rainey. But even though a few of his songs had been published and he had established a name as one of the Windy City's up-and-coming blues artists, he could not find any personal peace.

For Dorsey, a man who had grown up in a deeply religious family, living a life in the shadows brought a sense of shame. He hid that discomfort from friends by claiming that the blues and jazz were so much engrained in his soul that he had to hit the gin joints and night clubs. It was the only way he could fully express himself. He argued that being a part of this kind of music scene, where there were few rules and improvisation was demanded, gave him the opportunity to grow. In truth, he was as restless as the winds blowing off Lake Michigan. Finally, when drowning his sorrows in the vices his father preached against offered no relief, Dorsey considered suicide. On a cold winter night, with thoughts of death haunting his every step, he wandered into a church and, through the music more than the message, was reintroduced to God. Leaving the pew, he returned home and penned a gospel song, "If You See My Savior, Tell Him That You Saw Me."

This composition, like Dorsey's work in blues and jazz, was autobiographical. This song about a deathbed visit with a dying man was inspired by personal experience and drawn straight from the heart. It was also revolutionary in that even the lyrics about going to heaven reflected strains of the blues. And the mournful, plaintive words were coupled with musical riffs just like those Dorsey was playing in night clubs.

While writing "If You See My Savior, Tell Him That You Saw Me" helped Dorsey refocus his life and give up drinking, it did not help his career. Even in Chicago, which was much more liberal than the South, the church music establishment and publishing industry saw Dorsey's gospel song as having too much of a blues influence to be used in worship services. Some even called his approach to hymns a vehicle for the devil to gain entrance into the church. The songwriter was devastated. He was a man ready to give his life to Christian music but who found no one willing to offer him work.

Because he was married, Dorsey had no choice but to take any job he could find. That meant going back to the night clubs. Yet even as he played the blues in smoky bars, he refused to give up on the new style of Christian music he was developing. It would take an evolution in black churches to finally provide Dorsey with a break.

During the 1920s, African Americans had begun pushing for equality. In that era, one of the methods black Americans used to try to prove their value was adopting the style and tone found in white America. This concept even invaded the ways some African American churches conducted services. Tossing old Negro spirituals to the side, many black congregations used traditional European hymns on Sunday mornings. While the services were impressive in presentation, some younger members felt they lacked soul. Over time, the youth, who had been raised on blues, began to demand music that spoke to them. That opened a door for Dorsey's mix of gospel and jazz.

Taking his original material, he adapted and arranged it for choirs, and thanks to young black Christians, suddenly Chicago's African American churches were awash in Dorsey's new blend of traditional gospel themes enhanced by strains lifted from the blues. As news of the composer's new style swept the nation, he was offered the opportunity to travel across the Midwest and the South. In 1932, he was in St. Louis, singing and conducting choirs at a music convention, when he received an urgent phone call. His wife had gone into premature labor, and she and the baby were in serious condition. Climbing into his car, Dorsey hurried back to Chicago, but before he arrived, his wife was dead. A day later, his child died. This double tragedy brought Dorsey to his knees. After praying at his late wife's bedside, he rose, walked to the piano, and in a matter of minutes put his grief to music. He sang "Blessed Lord, Take My Hand" at the funeral services, then, before it was published, changed the lyrics to "Precious Lord, Take My Hand."

While his wife's death cost Dorsey dearly, the song his loss inspired quickly emerged as the most popular African American choral standard of the decade. In performances, to which thousands flocked to hear Dorsey, he was now backed by some of the greatest choirs in the nation. Though written and intended for African American audiences, his blues-based sacred music was quickly accepted and adopted by white churches. His new style also influenced scores of composers of all races and laid the framework for the youth-oriented Christian songs that began to appear two decades later.

Seven years after his wife's death, Dorsey, now recognized as one of the most respected voices in the black community, was traveling by train. As he sat in a car reserved for people of his race, he glanced out the window. He would later explain to a gathering of newspaper reporters what he saw that day:

It was just before Hitler sent his war chariots into Western Europe. I was on a train going through southern Indiana on the way to Cincinnati, and the country seemed to be upset about this coming war that Hitler was about to bring on. I passed through a valley on the train. Horses, cows, and

sheep were all grazing together in this little valley. A little
brook was running through the valley, and up the hill there I
could see where the water was falling. Everything seemed so
peaceful with all the animals down there grazing together. It
made me wonder what's the matter with humanity? What's
the matter with mankind? Why couldn't man live in peace
like the animals down there?[1]

Even as the train continued its journey, Dorsey pulled out
pen and paper and wrote what was on his heart. He had
just recently taught a choir an old Negro spiritual, and his
new melody echoed the field songs once sung by slaves. He
then infused his tune with a bit of blues and white hillbilly
music before wrapping it in a message that simply asked why
people couldn't seem to get along with one another on earth.

When Dorsey finished his latest composition, "Peace in
the Valley" had a very personal feel. Though it was universal
in its message, it also pulled greatly from Dorsey's experiences as a black man living in a world filled with prejudice.
To him, and millions of others, life was simply not fair.
There were few opportunities, and each day was a struggle.
His lyrics suggested that real peace could be found only in
two ways. The first was by fully embracing Christ and his
message. The other was by escaping the world through death
and living in the perfection of heaven.

"Peace in the Valley" became one of the most popular
religious songs performed during World War II. It crossed

all color lines and was adopted by almost every denomination. With bullets flying and bombs falling, its haunting lyrics became one of the nation's most powerful musical prayers. It was used at bond rallies as a prayer, in churches as a call to accept Jesus, and in funerals as a final goodbye. When the war was over and peace seemed at hand, the song began to fade from public consciousness. It might have been lost altogether except for a single performance on January 6, 1957. With more than fifty million watching, a man who had found a way to successfully blend black and white music performed on *The Ed Sullivan Show*. That night Elvis Presley asked viewers to give money to the Red Cross to help two hundred and fifty thousand Hungarian refugees fleeing a Soviet invasion. To emphasize the appeal, he sang "Peace in the Valley." Thanks to that performance, more than six million dollars were raised and millions flocked to record stores to buy Presley's first gospel record, which included two Dorsey compositions.

Thomas Dorsey died in 1993. Naturally, his greatest gospel composition was played at his funeral. Even as many of his friends and admirers cried, Dorsey was already experiencing a peace that was all but impossible to find on earth and seeing with his own eyes the beast of the wild led by a child.

To learn more about Thomas A. Dorsey, read Robert L. Taylor's *Thomas A. Dorsey, Father of Black Gospel Music: An Interview: Genesis of Black Gospel Music*, published by Trafford Publishing in 2014.

We're Marching to Zion

The LORD's ransomed ones will return and enter
    Zion with singing,
  with everlasting joy upon their heads.
Happiness and joy will overwhelm them;
  grief and groaning will flee away.

Isaiah 35:10

Come, we that love the Lord, and let our joys be
    known,
  Join in a song with sweet accord,
  join in a song with sweet accord
  And thus surround the throne,
  and thus surround the throne.

Refrain:
We're marching to Zion, beautiful, beautiful Zion.
We're marching upward to Zion, the beautiful city
    of God.

Let those refuse to sing who never knew our God;
But children of the heavenly King,
but children of the heavenly King
May speak their joys abroad,
may speak their joys abroad.

The hill of Zion yields a thousand sacred sweets
Before we reach the heavenly fields,
before we reach the heavenly fields
Or walk the golden streets,
or walk the golden streets.

Then let our songs abound, and every tear be dry.
We're marching through Immanuel's ground,
we're marching through Immanuel's ground
To fairer worlds on high,
to fairer worlds on high.

Almost three and a half centuries ago, an English family had just returned from church and was gathered around the table for Sunday dinner. As the meal progressed, talk turned to what had taken place during the worship service. A teenage boy listened intently as his father gave some viewpoints on the message. When the elder man concluded, the boy noted, "Father, it was boring."

In almost any other English household of that time, the son would have found himself in deep trouble. But Isaac Watts Sr. was more amused than upset. After all, in an act of rebellion, the elder Watts had recently left the Church of England and joined the new Congregationalist movement. And he didn't exit quietly; he spoke out against the Anglican Church in such a dramatic fashion that he was jailed for several months. Yet on this Sunday afternoon, as he studied his son, also named Isaac, Watts smiled and posed a question: "Why was it boring?"

The teen explained that they sang only from the book of Psalms, and they matched those words with just a half dozen tunes. Hence, no one really paid any attention or showed any enthusiasm. Not only did the young people hate it, but in truth, the older folks did too. Over the next few minutes, Isaac continued to explain the reactions of people to the music and then stated his opinion that church should be a place of joy but instead had become a few hours of weekly tedium. That was a pretty strong critique of a service his father had helped organize and lead!

Most parents, even today, likely would have explained to their child why things needed to stay the way they had always been. They would have talked about traditions and the importance of unveiling Scripture the way that David had with a harp and a tune. But the elder Watts remained silent as he considered Isaac's observations. He knew his son well; even as a very young child, the boy had written poems. The father was also fully aware that the brilliant young Isaac had read the Bible not just in English but also in Greek. In fact, though just a teen, Isaac was able to understand Latin and Hebrew as well. So rather than give the standard "you need to respect the way things are done" lecture, he issued a challenge.

"Son, if you think you can do better, then do it." Before the day was over, Isaac had penned "Behold the Glories of the Lamb."

With his father's encouragement, Isaac taught his new song to the church choir. When it was performed during the next Sunday morning service, the congregation was aghast. They had never experienced anything like it. Rather than demand the boy be punished for blasphemy, however, they asked to hear "Behold the Glories of the Lamb" again. Without realizing it, that little church had set in motion a monumental change in worship.

The move to singing songs not taken directly from the Bible was not without controversy. Many churches split over this new kind of music. Many felt that singing songs penned by commoners was a part of Satan's plan to corrupt young people. Even being called an advocate for the devil didn't keep Isaac from continuing to pen new hymns, and his church became a radical beacon for a fresh style of praise and worship.

In 1701, after completing college, Isaac Watts became the lead minister at the Mark Lane Independent Chapel in London. He remained at the church until his death forty-seven years later. People from across the city flocked to hear Watts preach, but most left with a far better understanding of faith as learned through his original music. Just as he had suggested to his father years before, messages personalized and presented in music really awakened the soul. But though Watts had become one of the most talked about Christian leaders in England, his life was far from perfect.

Six years after assuming his role as pastor, a lonely and discouraged Watts walked into his church office. He had begun his day with great hopes, but his spirit had been crushed by a woman who had rejected his marriage proposal. Her reason for turning him down had nothing to do with Watts's heart. Instead, she told him he was too ugly to be her husband.

As he paced, Watts glanced into the mirror and frowned. Due to a childhood bout with smallpox, pock marks and scars covered his face. On top of that, his nose was hooked, his lips were thin, and he was barely five feet tall. He wondered how anyone but God could love a man such as he.

Turning his face from the mirror, he sat at his desk, opened his Bible, and tried to find some type of comfort in the Scriptures he knew so well. But on this day, the stories of Job, Moses, and Jesus could not lift him out of his depression. At a loss for how to escape his overwhelming feelings of rejection, he picked up a pen. Over the course of several hours, the preacher composed eleven verses of poetry. The words reflected his deep faith in God and his calling as well as the state of his heart after suffering such a great rejection.

The beginning of the song conveyed God's love and the joy of serving him. But after that optimistic beginning, Watts plunged into the sadness of the moment. In many of the lines, he revealed his disappointment and loneliness.

> Come, we that love the Lord,
> And let our joys be known;
> Join in a song with sweet accord,
> And thus surround the throne.

> The sorrows of the mind
> Be banish'd from the place!
> Religion never was design'd
> To make our pleasures less.

As his work continued, he threw off the cross of ugliness he felt was his to bear and began to consider the happiness found in serving God. He also examined the power God had over everything in this often sad world.

> Let those refuse to sing
> That never knew our God,
> But favourites of the heavenly King
> May speak their joys abroad.

> The God that rules on high,
> And thunders when he please,
> That rides upon the stormy sky
> And manages the seas.

> This awful God is ours,
> Our Father and our love,

He shall send down his heavenly powers
To carry us above.

Watts finally went from earth to heaven. In the next verse, he wrote of the amazing moment when he would see God face-to-face. At that instant, all ugliness would end and perfection would begin. Throughout the remainder of his newest work, he embraced the triumph of love over hate, and grace and redemption over rejection and condemnation. His final message was that no matter what others thought of him, God loved him so much that he was going to provide Watts with a home that was beyond imagination.

There we shall see his face,
And never, never sin;
There from the rivers of his grace
Drink endless pleasures in.

Yes, and before we rise
To that immortal state,
The thoughts of such amazing bliss
Should constant joys create.

The men of grace have found
Glory begun below,
Celestial fruits on earthly ground
From faith and hope may grow.

The hill of Sion yields
A thousand sacred sweets,

147

Before we reach the heavenly fields,
Or walk the golden streets.

Then let our songs abound,
And every tear be dry;
We're marching thro' Immanuel's ground
To fairer worlds on high.

Throughout the course of his life, Watts would pen such immortal hymns as "When I Survey the Wondrous Cross," "Joy to the World," and "O God, Our Help in Ages Past." From the moment each of those works was published, they were embraced and loved. And yet his hymn born out of a failed marriage proposal would not become widely known during his lifetime. It would take two more men and a name change to make "Come, We that Love the Lord" one of the most revered songs in history.

John Wesley often studied the writings and music of Isaac Watts. In the 1700s, John and his brother Charles built their work on the foundation Watts had laid. When Wesley stumbled across "Come, We that Love the Lord" in an old hymnal, he liked it but felt it incomplete. So years after Watts had penned the song about heaven, the man who founded the Methodist movement cut some of the original verses and rewrote and added a few lines. He also changed the spelling of "Sion" to the more modern "Zion." While not fully satisfied, Wesley published his version and then moved to other hymns.

A century later, an American Baptist preacher, Robert Lowry, studied both Watts's and Wesley's versions of "Come, We that Love the Lord." While he thought the lyrics in both arrangements were strong, he decided the words were mated to the wrong melody. After cutting a few more verses, he started looking for a modern tune that might make the song acceptable to a new generation. At that time, Americans were fascinated with march music. With that in mind, Lowry penned a new chorus and set it to a melody he called "Marching to Zion." The fresh music and added refrain reshaped the entire song and transformed it from a traditional British-style hymn into an up-tempo anthem. While in the past others had dismissed the song as being melancholy, in its new form, "We're Marching to Zion" reflected a victory over heartache, suffering, and death. The march theme also trumpeted a gathering of believers forming a spiritual army inspired not by war but by love. Thus came the irony seen so often in church music: a song written by a man who had been rejected by a suitor became a hymn that fully embraced the joys of God's love for his children.

Without Isaac Watts, there might not have been a revolution in church music. Responding to his father's challenge, he opened the door for Christians to pen songs reflecting their faith and experiences. In that way, these new, personal Christian compositions became testimonies that could be shared in a corporate worship setting. Still, among the hundreds he composed, a song inspired by a lost dream gave the world perhaps its most uplifting and exciting picture of heaven. In the midst of sadness and rejection, the great writer marched on and found a way to inspire joy and faith.

To learn more about Isaac Watts, read Douglas Bond's *The Poetic Wonder of Isaac Watts*, published by Reformation Trust Publishing in 2013, or Graham Beynon's *Isaac Watts: His Life and Thought*, published by Christian Focus in 2013.

This World Is
Not My Home

We don't have a permanent city here, but rather we are looking for the city that is still to come.

Hebrews 13:14

B. W. B. Masterson, known as Bat to his friends, had
seen a great deal in his life. Born in Canada in 1853,
he moved to the American Great Plains as a child. Over the
next few decades, he worked on the railroad, served as an
army scout, spent time as a buffalo hunter, became a noted
gunfighter, and then was elected sheriff in Dodge City, Kansas. He continued in law enforcement for a few years before
leaping into theater management. He then left the West and
headed to New York to take on the role of a fight promoter.
In that same location, he moved into his final occupation:
writing. Over the last two decades of his life, Masterson was
one of the best-known sport scribes in America.

On the morning of October 12, 1921, the always dapper sixty-three-year-old Masterson was sitting at his desk at the *New York Morning Telegram* working on an opinion column. As he considered the state of the world, he penned these words: "There are those who argue that everything breaks even in this old dump of a world of ours. I suppose these ginks who argue that way hold that, because the rich man gets ice in the summer and the poor man gets it in the winter, things are breaking even for both. Maybe so, but I'll swear I can't see it that way."[1] Just as he completed those final thoughts, he was felled by a heart attack. He never wrote or said another word, and his last column remained unfinished.

What Masterson noted was that, for most, life wasn't fair. He had watched Native Americans be all but wiped out and those who survived moved to lands no one wanted. He had seen countless pioneers taken advantage of by robber barons and land speculators and had observed powerful men run roughshod over the poor of every color. He had seen children work twelve hours a day in factories for a few cents an hour and had watched women beg in the streets after their husbands had died in wars or industrial accidents. In life, just as in the boxing matches he covered, more often than not, the biggest won and the weakest lost. So in his final words, one of the legends of the American West noted the dynamic of an earthly existence that was anything but fair.

Albert E. Brumley and Bat Masterson could not have been more different. While Masterson haunted speakeasies and played cards in gambling halls, Brumley sang hymns in churches and original gospel songs on the radio. Yet even though their backgrounds were extremely different, they both used words to describe the events and circumstances they witnessed. And from their vastly different prose came the stories of people who had been pushed around, taken advantage of, and walked on.

Brumley's style of writing mirrored that of legendary country music song scribe Hank Williams. Both men were able to take complex thoughts and ideas and explain them in simple phrases. While Williams usually focused on the pain and in some cases the joy found in a poor man's life, Brumley centered on the hope found in a Christian life. And the gospel music writer, unlike his country counterpart, also found a way to wrap life experiences into a package that revealed the joy of living even in an unfair world. He didn't bring sad people down; he found ways to lift them up out of the depths of despair.

Brumley had lived through two major world wars and the Great Depression. He had witnessed families ripped apart by disease and prejudice. He knew the fragility of life as well as the suffering caused by poverty. For those who had lost loved ones or could not find a way to climb out of an economic hole, he felt a call to provide hope. Therefore, a great number of his songs centered on the rewards of faith. In his catalogue of work, his most loved compositions all put the spotlight on heaven.

In 1946, Brumley, as was his daily habit, sat down in his office to write. One of the questions he was most often asked concerned why life was so unfair. Why was it that good men had to suffer so? Brumley, before establishing a profitable career in music, had worked on a farm and in a store. He knew what it was like to make less than a dollar a day. When he was starting out, he passed by mansions on his way to his modest home. As he grew older, he came to the conclusion that, just like the children of Israel, most found getting to the promised land a very difficult trek. The only way to make it there was to keep going. And as he considered those thoughts, something dawned on him. The earth was much like the desert the children of Israel wandered in for forty years, and heaven was the promised land. In other words, life in this world was just a transitory period, while death was a bridge to a refreshing place of perfection and joy. With that thought in mind, Brumley created four verses and a chorus in just a few minutes. In his new song, he suggested that life's wealth was not found in today's money and possessions but in the rewards of grace.

While in his new song Brumley painted a beautiful picture of heaven, it was really secondary to the point he was trying to emphasize. "This World Is Not My Home" fully embraced the theme that Jesus was not just a Savior but a friend. Thus, Brumley spotlighted the benefits of a spiritual relationship with God on earth as much as the promise of being with the Lord in heaven. This positive theme of faith in the face of often overwhelming odds proved universal. "This World Is

Not My Home" was recorded by artists in country, gospel, and blues as well as arranged into choral anthems.

The formula Christ gave for happiness involved service to God by serving others. The great missionary doctor Albert Schweitzer lived by that edict. On December 3, 1935, when speaking to students at Ackworth School, he said, "I don't know what your destiny will be, but one thing I know, the only ones among you who will be really happy are those who have sought and found how to serve."

In truth, if we have only one life, then Schweitzer's words are without meaning. If this earthly existence is all we are given, perhaps we should live in the moment, grab what we can, and not worry about who we hurt to get our share. But if amassing wealth is all there is to life, then when life is finished, so is its value. There has to be more!

When Bat Masterson penned his final words, they came out as a hopeless snapshot of life in New York City. In his view, for the poor, existence was futile and devastating. Yet Schweitzer and Brumley knew better. Daily life has purpose and hope found in serving God in this life so we can celebrate with him in the next. And as can be seen in "This World Is Not My Home," if this life isn't fair, that's fine, because as the song says, "This world is not my home, I'm just passing through, my treasures are laid up, somewhere beyond the blue." The next life will be amazing!

I'll Fly Away

This is because the Lord himself will come down from heaven with the signal of a shout by the head angel and a blast on God's trumpet. First, those who are dead in Christ will rise.

1 Thessalonians 4:16

Born in 1905 outside the tiny town of Spiro, Oklahoma, Albert Brumley arrived on this earth at just the right moment to see a world transforming at light speed. Never in history had civilization been so consumed by change and innovation. When Brumley was growing up, it seemed as though something impossible was invented every day. So when he graduated from high school, the landscape looked much different than it had just two decades before, and everyone was convinced it was for the better. Many were calling the Jazz Age the greatest time in history. It was as if inspiration had been set free and was soaring.

In 1924, when the wide-eyed farm boy became a student studying music under Eugene Bartlett, the United States was the most optimistic place on earth. Thanks to what was then known as the Great War, the nation had emerged as a superpower and a world leader. Fueled by the Industrial Revolution, the stock market was booming. Higher wages meant the middle class was growing and fewer people were living in poverty. Telephones were becoming common, connecting people in a way no other invention in history had done. Radio instantly brought news and entertainment to every corner of the country. And the nation had taken to the air, with planes transporting freight and passengers faster than most people could imagine. And it was the airplane, much more than any other invention, that fascinated Americans. For the first time, it was possible for people to escape gravity.

Brumley, like almost everyone else in the nation in those days, looked skyward each time he heard an airborne engine. As he studied planes in flight, he dreamed of navigating the clouds. In his mind, the freest person in the world was the one who could jump into a plane and leave the earth behind.

When he arrived at the Hartford Music Institute, a school devoted to teaching talented and creative people how to compose gospel music, Brumley was little more than a naïve farm boy. He had grown up in a sheltered environment and had traveled little. While he knew the Bible from cover to cover, he was completely innocent in the ways of the world. Thus, every new experience, from ice-cream sodas to movies that talked, left him slack jawed. Other students, who had been to large cities and felt more sophisticated due to their brushes with modern culture, enjoyed poking fun at the bumpkin from the Oklahoma plains. He quickly became the butt of many jokes. At first, they just rolled off his back. But in time, they got under his skin.

Beyond his fascination with the ever-changing world, Brumley was captivated by angels. These heavenly creatures who seemed to possess wisdom and incomprehensible physical powers fired his imagination. He never grew tired of reading about their winging their way from heaven to earth in an attempt to guide lost or confused souls. The imagery of angels and their connection to heaven inspired and shaped many of the more than five hundred songs he composed during his seventy-two years of life.

Brumley had gone to Hartford to study with Bartlett because he saw gospel music as a voice of Christian optimism. He honestly felt a saved soul should create a happy person. So he believed his compositions should reflect this optimistic nature. Ironically, when he penned his initial song about heaven, his positive view of faith crashed and burned.

At the end of his first year of school, Brumley and his classmates were asked to write something completely original. When it came his time to debut his assignment, Brumley was excited. He thought he had penned the next big gospel music hit. When the other students heard "I Can Hear Them

Singing Over There," they laughed. They suggested that all he had done was slightly rework the music and lyrics of a familiar Eugene Bartlett song. Humbled, embarrassed, and hurt, feeling like a complete failure, Brumley packed his bags and moved back to his family farm for the summer vacation.

Everyone assumed that Brumley would return to Hartford for the fall semester. Yet on the day he was supposed to leave, the young man picked up a hoe and began weeding a cotton patch. Vowing to never again place himself in a situation in which he would face ridicule and criticism, he packed away his long-held dream of being a songwriter and committed to working the soil.

While he was able to leave school, he wasn't able to free himself from the draw of music. It was forever rooted in his heart and stuck in his head. On a hot fall day, as Brumley walked the long rows of a cotton field, he began to sing the number one song on the hit parade. Little did he know that this moment would redefine the rest of his life. Ironically, he never met the man who provided the vehicle to get his life back on track, but they had something in common. Vernon Dalhart was also someone who had a few doors slammed in his face.

Texas-born Dalhart had long dreamed of singing opera, but a series of rejections forced him to look in other directions. At the very moment classical music showed Dalhart the door, the record industry was booming. Talent scouts were going coast to coast and border to border searching for singers to record the latest compositions from New York's Tin Pan Alley song scribes. Dalhart not only had the voice and stage presence for the job but also could sing any style. Simply by being in the right place at the right time, he established himself as a vocalist, and as his records began to climb the charts, the singer expanded into publishing. One of his first discoveries was a song penned by a relative who had once spent time in prison. In just a few simple verses, Robert Massey proved he had a deep insight into the tortured minds of those spending years behind bars.

Massey's "The Prisoner Song" was a hopeless ballad written from the point of view of a man facing life without the chance of parole. In the song's lyrics, the sight of a bird landing in the prison yard and then taking flight over the walls caused the prisoner to wish he had wings so he could fly too. Dalhart's recording was considered one of the first country music hits.

As Brumley sang "The Prisoner Song," he stopped and studied the flat ground he was working. While there were no concrete barriers or guard towers, like the prisoner in the hit song, he was serving a life sentence. He had created his own prison by giving up on what he believed God had called him to do. That night while sitting at a table, he tried to rework the concept of Dalhart's sad ode into a joyful, upbeat song about being freed from the bonds of a hopeless world by grace. While the idea was strong, Brumley couldn't get his concept off the ground. But the idea wouldn't leave him alone. It haunted him week after week and month after month.

For the next few years, each time he saw a bird fly, Brumley stopped to work on "I'll Fly Away." Each of these writing sessions ended in frustration. He always made a good start, but he didn't have the tools to finish his work. The fact that his best idea remained grounded caused Brumley to reexamine a life that had in fact become a prison. He came to realize that the only way he would have the opportunity for parole would be to go back to Bartlett and ask for a second chance.

In 1929, Brumley wrote a letter and requested readmittance to the Hartford Music Institute. As he did not have the money for tuition, room, or board, he also had to admit he needed help. Bartlett, who still believed in Brumley's raw talent, offered free schooling in exchange for his singing with the Hartford Quartet and traveling across the South selling songbooks and magazines. The farmer jumped at the opportunity.

For the next six years, Brumley worked for Bartlett. With the older man's guidance, Brumley's ability to create original material grew to the point where he finally felt confident enough to dig out an almost forgotten idea. A decade after singing "The Prisoner's Song" in a cotton field, the idea finally took wings and became a new song. Bartlett's company, Hartford Publishing, placed "I'll Fly Away" in the company's latest hymnal.

In a world awash in suffering, Brumley's new take on making the journey from a painful existence on earth to a place where suffering was unknown and joy was everywhere struck a chord. Within months of its release, "I'll Fly Away" became the hottest-selling song in Hartford Publishing's extensive catalogue. On top of that, scores of acts recorded it.

Having a hit should have paved the way for Brumley's career to soar, but it didn't. His agreement with Bartlett meant the publisher owned all the rights to anything Brumley created. Thus, Brumley received no royalties for "I'll Fly Away" and had to continue to make ends meet on his fifteen-dollar-a-week salary. Ironically, the song that almost caused the Oklahoman to give up on writing now paved his way to independence.

With the incredible success of "I'll Fly Away," Hartford Publishing released Brumley's first song about heaven, "I Can Hear Them Singing Over There." The royalties generated by this hymn allowed Brumley to create his own publishing company and begin to write full time. "Turn Your Radio On," "I'll Meet You in the Morning," "If We Never Meet Again," and "I Just Steal Away and Pray" soon pushed Brumley ahead of Bartlett as gospel music's most successful songwriter.

Medical science has progressed to the point where many people who have been ruled clinically dead have been brought back to life. Some of those who died but were revived have told stories of flying out of their bodies. They have also reported a sense of peace and joy that fully enveloped them while in the air. In a very real way, these firsthand accounts of life after death parallel the lyrics of "I'll Fly Away."

Though Bartlett would eventually make hundreds of thousands of dollars from "I'll Fly Away," Brumley never complained about his business deal with his mentor. After all, Bartlett had not only offered the way out of a life Brumley considered a prison but also taught him the skills necessary to take an idea that was going nowhere and give it wings.

To learn more about Albert Brumley, read his autobiography written with Kay Hively, *I'll Fly Away*, published by Mountaineer Books in 1990.

The Unclouded Day

Then, we who are living and still around will be taken up together with them in the clouds to meet with the Lord in the air. That way we will always be with the Lord.

1 Thessalonians 4:17

Oh, they tell me of a home far beyond the skies,
Oh, they tell me of a home far away;
Oh, they tell me of a home where no storm clouds rise,
Oh, they tell me of an unclouded day.

Refrain:
Oh, the land of cloudless day,
Oh, the land of an unclouded sky,
Oh, they tell me of a home where no storm clouds rise,
Oh, they tell me of an unclouded day.

Oh, they tell me of a home where my friends have gone,
Oh, they tell me of that land far away,

Where the tree of life in eternal bloom
Sheds its fragrance through the unclouded day.

Oh, they tell me of a King in His beauty there,
And they tell me that mine eyes shall behold
Where He sits on the throne that is whiter than snow,
In the city that is made of gold.

Oh, they tell me that He smiles on His children there,
And His smile drives their sorrows all away;
And they tell me that no tears ever come again
In that lovely land of unclouded day.

*O*ne of the world's most popular phone apps provides constantly updating weather reports. With a few taps, cell phone owners can check detailed forecasts for their location or for anywhere else on the planet. On the web, weather sites are used as often as email. And cable weather channels garner higher ratings than many television movie networks. We live in a world that is obsessed with knowing the weather, and the fact is that this obsession is nothing new. Weather has always fascinated and frightened people.

For thousands of years, when clouds began to roll in and become dark and threatening, eyes turned toward the sky. Since the beginning of time, people have known that on any given day, clouds can produce damaging winds, hail, tornados, and rain. In many cases, what follows is destruction and misery.

Traveling in a storm can be brutal and dangerous. If a person is driving, every sense is challenged. If they are walking, bad weather can make their trek both dangerous and miserable. Dark clouds can spawn chaos, and that chaos can lead to suffering and even death. No one knew that fact more than Josiah Alwood.

Alwood was born in Harrison County, Ohio, in 1828. As a boy, Alwood became fascinated with reading and spent hours studying the Bible. He was especially drawn to the stories of the apostle Paul. He often imagined the difficulties Paul must have encountered on his journeys. In fact, Alwood's admiration for the apostle's missionary work was so great that his parents were not surprised when Josiah told his church he wanted to be a missionary. Ordained in his late teens by the United Brethren of Christ, Alwood volunteered for the most dangerous and challenging of Christian work. While most preachers asked for individual churches, he took on the nomadic role of a modern Paul.

Circuit-riding preachers were an integral part of early American life. Assigned to as many as eight churches at a time, these men would ride for hours, give a Sunday morning message, and then climb back on their horse for an often arduous trip of many more miles to give a second sermon. Most of these small congregations met once a month, and a large percentage of these rural American Christians couldn't read. Thus, the circuit rider's messages were their only exposure to the gospel.

As Alwood traveled through Michigan and Ohio, the America that greeted him was a dangerous place. People were suspicious of most travelers, even those who dressed like the clergy and carried a Bible. The roads were little more than trails, and the law was based less on what was found in books and more on who had the most power. Robbers were common, and homes that welcomed strangers were rare. And in the areas where Alwood was assigned, churchgoing Christians were not in the majority. Many pioneers saw little use for men who claimed they could lead them to a spiritual life. Because the job was so dangerous, demeaning, and demanding and the pay was so low, many circuit riders lasted only a few years before giving up.

For four decades, Alwood filled the role of the traveling pastor. He sometimes went weeks without seeing his home or his family, and on most days, his only companion was his horse. He often ate what he could fish out of streams or shoot in the woods. On many nights, he slept out in the open on hard ground. Still, the worst part of his life was the weather. Alwood was forced to ride in rain and snow. He faced the heat of summer and the brutal cold of Midwestern winters. There were times when he had ice in his beard and his feet were all but frozen. Other days the rain beat down so hard that he was soaked to the skin. Though he faced all these challenges alone, his call was so strong that he just kept riding.

On a Sunday night in August 1879, the fifty-one-year-old pastor finished a service at a small Ohio church. His circuit was over, and it was time to go back home to his family in Michigan. On this night, several members caught him before he could rush out the door. For the next hour, the small group peppered the preacher with questions about everything from his views on the weather to heaven. Only after he led them in a time of prayer did the meeting break up. Then an exhausted Alwood climbed onto his horse and began an all-night journey toward home.

When traveling in daylight, the preacher would often pull out his Bible and read. At night, that was impossible. Tired and lonely, he stayed awake by looking back over his career. Perhaps due to the darkness, he began to question if giving his life to the ministry had been a mistake. Even though he was aware the members of the churches he served loved him, it was also abundantly clear he was not making much impact in the small communities where he preached. He couldn't remember the last time someone had walked the aisle to give their life to Christ. In fact, on most Sundays, only regulars strolled through the church doors. When compared to his hero Paul, he appeared to be accomplishing nothing. At that moment, it seemed the only thing the two men had in common was a belief in Jesus and roads filled with hardships.

As he continued to ride, a bright moon rose, its light providing the illumination he needed to pick up his pace. About an hour later, he saw something that took his breath away. Alwood yanked the reins, rubbed his eyes, and pulled out his pocket watch. It was midnight, and yet just in front of him was a rainbow. How was that possible? In 1896, in a self-penned article called "A Rainbow at Midnight and a Song in the Morning," featured in the *Christian Conservator*, Alwood told the story of what he witnessed.

> It was a balmy night in August 1879, when returning from Spring Hill, Ohio, to my home in Morenci, Michigan, about 1:00 a.m. I saw a beautiful rainbow north by northwest against a dense black nimbus cloud. The sky was all perfectly clear except this dark cloud which covered about forty degrees of the horizon and extended about halfway to the zenith. The phenomenon was entirely new to me and my nerves refreshed by the balmy air and the lovely sight.[1]

As tired and as sleepy as he was, Alwood was suddenly filled with an incredible energy and enthusiasm. Both excited and inspired, Alwood, over the course of his long journey home, wrote a poem called "A Rainbow at Night and a Song in the Morning." He initially figured it would serve as the basis for a Sunday morning message, but when he walked inside his house, the idea was transformed. A melody had been playing in Alwood's mind since witnessing the midnight rainbow. When he sat down at the organ and played the simple tune, he realized it fit perfectly with his poem. Though he had not intended to, he had written a song.

After polishing his work, he played it for his family. It was then that he realized God had given him the rainbow as much more than a preview of heaven; it was a sign that his life had been of great value. He had ridden through all kinds of weather and experienced great misery while serving God, but doing so had been worth it. He had touched lives and led people to the Lord. And in time, they would all end up at the same home together. Hence, the song now known as "The Unclouded Day" was the story of his life.

For the next decade, Alwood used his song to share his vision of heaven. In time, as his small congregations learned "The Unclouded Day," they sang it at the end of services as a way of saying goodbye to the circuit-riding preacher, but outside the circuit, it was unknown. Finally, in 1890, "The Unclouded Day" was published and within twenty years was being sung across the Midwest. Still, Alwood's musical autobiography would not become widely popular until the advent of the gospel quartet movement in the 1920s. By then, Alwood was already experiencing the unclouded days of heaven firsthand.

As Josiah Alwood rode from church to church, he had to deal with the unpredictability of the weather. There can be little doubt that his experiences with heat and cold and rain and snow helped him create his song of hope. Still, for most, the storms of life are unexpected deaths, betrayals, disease, financial challenges, and loneliness. For them, "The Unclouded Day" serves as a reminder that while life on earth is often stormy, the next life is much different. Death is not an end but a ticket to a home where "no storm clouds rise" and no weather apps are needed.

Walk Dem Golden Stairs

I assure you that whoever hears my word and believes in the one who sent me has eternal life and won't come under judgment but has passed from death into life.

John 5:24

Though Jesus was Jewish by birth, his message was all-inclusive and his teachings were meant for men and women of all ages and ethnic backgrounds. In a very real sense, Christ showed that God's love is equal and given unconditionally. It's not just for a select few; it's not meant for only white, black, yellow, or brown but for everyone. And one of the most loved songs about heaven was introduced by a group who mirrored the colorlessness of faith.

Unlike in the 1890s, in the days after World War II, barbershop quartets didn't sell many records or draw huge concert crowds. Singing in one was not the way to fame or wealth. In fact, for those who performed the barbershop harmonies, it was seen as a hobby, not a profession. Yet a group that began singing barbershop for fun would go on to be featured on more recordings than any other voices in history.

In 1948, in Springfield, Missouri, the Foggy Mountain Boys lost two of their members and considered breaking up. When brothers Monty and Bill Matthews were discussing the group's future, they ran into Bob Hubbard and Hoyt Hawkins. Just for fun, the two members of the old quartet sang a few numbers with their new friends. They sounded so good on barbershop numbers that they opted to keep singing. Due to the limited appeal of the barbershop style, they added a bit of gospel music to their act and renamed themselves the Jordanaires after a local creek.

The quartet performed in churches for several months. When they landed a few gigs on Missouri-based radio shows, things looked bright. But just as the Jordanaires were making a name for themselves, two members left. To fill the holes, the remaining members brought in a pair of graduates of the famed Stamps School of Music. After the additions of Gordon Stoker and Neal Matthews, the Jordanaires were invited to Nashville for an appearance on the *Grand Ole Opry*. That performance caught the attention of record executives, and the group was signed by Capitol Records. Their next step toward stardom was being picked as the back-up vocalists for country music's hottest star: Eddy Arnold. Thanks to that association, audiences across the nation were soon introduced to a sound many had never heard.

"What set us apart at that time," the late Gordon Stoker told me in 1999 while waiting to go on stage at a Patsy Cline tribute show in Las Vegas, "was that we sang spirituals. White quartets of the time just didn't sing black spirituals. We loved them, and our audiences did too. During our early years, some of our most requested numbers were 'Swing Low, Sweet Chariot,' 'Search Me, Lord,' and 'Joshua Fit the Battle of Jericho.' We even cut 'Peace in the Valley' before Red Foley recorded it."[1]

The white audiences that heard the Jordanaires with Arnold were not prepared for their sound. The quartet blend was not then a part of country music, and the fact that the group of white men sang black gospel music was almost shocking. But for the members of the Jordanaires, the songs were a natural extension of who they were. They had grown up listening to spirituals and often attended black churches. They saw this music as having a universal appeal. And they were proven right. The response was so great that the Jordanaires were invited to New York City for an appearance on *The Arthur Godfrey Show*. Stoker called it one of the highlights of the group's early days.

"We sang the old Negro spiritual 'Dig a Little Deeper.' That song literally stopped the show. Godfrey came over to the mic and said, 'Boys, I've never heard anything like that. I want you to sing again.' A little while later, we were called in to back up the wonderful Mahalia Jackson. She wanted us to sing with her. When we finished, she looked over at us almost in disbelief. She told the whole studio, 'I wanna sing with those boys again.' She did too!"

That appearance made the four men one of the best-known quartets in the country. But their *Godfrey Show* performance with Jackson hit an even deeper chord. Four white southern men had backed up a female African American performer. As this was a color line that likely had never been broken, it seemed revolutionary. It clearly showed that the Jordanaires were men who fully embraced Jesus's view of the world. In other words, all people are brothers and sisters in heaven and therefore should be on earth as well.

In 1955, while appearing with Eddy Arnold on the *Grand Ole Opry*, the quartet was approached by a young man dressed in a bright pink shirt and white coat. The all-but-unknown singer from Memphis wanted to tell the group how much he loved their sound. A year later, when RCA called and asked the Jordanaires to provide backup for a recording session, that same singer would dramatically alter their lives.

"From the very start we worked Elvis's sessions," Stoker explained. "When the sessions were over, we hung around and sang gospel songs for several more hours. Elvis's favorite music was gospel, and he loved to sing spirituals."

Elvis loved singing with the quartet so much that he took them everywhere. They were with him for his concerts and television appearances; they sang on his movie soundtracks and even appeared in his films. Though they had become the hottest backup group in the world, the Jordanaires still saw themselves as a gospel quartet. Even when appearing with secular acts at rock 'n' roll shows, when put in the spotlight, the quartet always sang songs that reflected their deep faith.

"Even though we were working with Elvis, Jim Reeves, Patsy Cline, Ernie Ford, Ricky Nelson, and a host of others," Stoker noted, "we were still cutting records of our own too. So although it seemed like it to a lot of people, we hadn't given up gospel. In fact, we were singing gospel music to more people than we ever had. We just weren't singing to the same audiences as the rest of the quartets at that time."

During one of their gospel music recording sessions, an idea for a song about heaven was born. It was a day Stoker would never forget.

"In one session, our bass singer, Cully Holt, began to talk to Monty Matthews about going to heaven. All day long Cully kept talking about walking the golden stairs to the pearly gates. Although he was not a songwriter, and to my knowledge never wrote another song, he went home and put words and music to his thoughts. When he was finished, he brought the song back to us. I knew when I first heard it that 'Walk Dem Golden Stairs' was great."

The new composition talked about the exhilaration that believers will experience during their journey to heaven. It also highlighted how much hearing Jesus call the travelers' names will mean. But for Stoker, what really made the song special was that it had the feel of an old Negro spiritual. Hence, the group was going back to its roots and getting to introduce a new number that mirrored the emotions found in hymns written by black slaves.

When "Walk Dem Golden Stairs" was released, gospel music crowds raced to record stores to buy it. It was so popular that it was quickly recorded by scores of white and black groups. Still, to gain an audience outside the rural South and become one of the best-known of all the songs focusing on heaven would take an accident and a bit of deception.

"When we were called in to do a gospel album with Elvis," Stoker explained, "we began to sing a little bit of 'Walk Dem Golden Stairs' to warm up. Elvis came over and as soon as he learned the words decided that he had to use it on the album we were cutting. I didn't believe it was going to happen. His manager, Tom Parker, had instructed RCA to use only songs that were in the public domain. He didn't want to have to pay any royalties to songwriters or publishers. I guess I should have spoken up and told Colonel Parker that Cully had written it and that Ben Speer Music owned the rights, but I decided to keep my mouth shut. I knew that Ben could use the money a lot more than Tom Parker."

The session began about sundown and went on past sunrise. It was what old-timers called an all-night gospel singing. As it broke up, Stoker called Speer on the phone. While Speer was excited that a song he owned had been recorded by Elvis, like Stoker, he was sure that Colonel Parker would cut it from the final release. Yet because "Walk Dem Golden Stairs" sounded so much like a Negro spiritual, no one at the label or in Parker's office ever checked on the rights. As a part of the award-winning and multimillion-selling *His Hand in Mine*, "Walk Dem Golden Stairs" became one of the world's most played gospel music songs.

In 2013, the Jordanaires sang for a final time. Within a year, all the original members of the Hall of Fame group made the walk up those golden stairs. Now the song that became their signature number serves as a reminder of Christ's message. The gospel is color-blind, and heaven is a place where all kinds of music blend together in a way that is only hinted at on earth.

Mansion over the Hilltop

My Father's house has room to spare. If that weren't the case, would I have told you that I'm going to prepare a place for you?

John 14:2

Even during the best weeks, there are disappointments in life. Fully living each day and counting each blessing require looking at the big picture. And sometimes when times are tough and it seems the whole world is against us, seeing beyond the clouds and finding the sunshine require the faith of a child. One of the greatest songs about the rewards promised in heaven was born in the illogical actions of a once disillusioned businessman and the heart of a little girl who had nothing. But first there had to be a meeting.

In the winter of 1945, the world was at peace for the first time in six years. For Americans who had been involved in the most destructive war the planet had ever seen, it was a day many feared would never come. When the Japanese surrendered and fathers, brothers, and sons laid down their guns, packed their footlockers, and headed home, it was a time of great celebration. For some, though, the realization that their loved ones were never coming home, that they had died while fighting for their country, meant the end of the war and the reunions that followed would be a sharp reality that was too painful to bear. In their world, the empty places would never be filled. Thus, it was a time of both happiness and heartache, of gain and loss, and of hope and despair.

In 1945, Ira Stanphill was a father and a husband who traveled the world as an evangelist. Outwardly, this great man of faith seemed to have all the answers. He spoke with authority, wrote songs that opened hearts, and had what looked like the perfect family. And yet just below the surface, his life was on the verge of collapse. While there might have been peace on earth, Stanphill was in a war to save his marriage. It was a battle he was fighting alone and losing. His wife had no interest in continuing to live with the preacher and had dreams far different from his. So he was trying to hold on to someone who couldn't wait to walk away and start over with someone else.

A disheartened and shaken Stanphill accepted an invitation to attend a Dallas revival meeting. As the service began, his focus was on his own pain. He sang songs, but the words didn't register, and he paid little attention as his friend, Reverend Gene Martin, introduced the speaker for the evening. It was only as the guest began to share his story that Stanphill snapped out of his fog.

The man standing in front of thousands that late fall night appeared to be in his sixties. His voice was strong and his demeanor humble. And as he unwound the story of his life, the audience was mesmerized. Leaning forward in the pew, Stanphill tuned in to what seemed to be the tale of a blessed life filled with great success. What he could not have guessed was that a dramatic detour was coming.

The speaker had once been one of the wealthiest men in Dallas. Thanks to his business and investments, he was able to build a huge home, drive the finest cars, and vacation at some of the nicest places on the planet. For a while, everything he touched seemed to turn to gold. And then, on a day in 1929, he lost millions of dollars in the stock market crash.

Over the next few years, the man watched his life and his dreams shrink. He was forced to sell his fleet of cars and his mansion, close many of his businesses, and say goodbye to very loyal employees. But cutting back didn't stop the bleeding, and try as hard as he could, he couldn't seem to turn things around. Within a few years, he was down to just a small operation with a few employees, and with sales tanking, no one had to tell him the end was in sight. It was starkly obvious that soon, like millions of other Americans mired in the Great Depression, he would have nothing, not even hope.

As the bad times grew worse and the end drew near, the businessman took what money he had in his pocket, filled his car with gas, and drove as fast as he could out of Dallas. He did not know where he was headed; he was just running from pain he couldn't handle and questions for which he had no answers. As the time passed and the miles stacked up, the roads went from pavement to gravel to dirt. With no map in the glove box, he soon realized he was lost. And he really didn't care.

As he looked through his windshield across the rural landscape, he noticed a small house that had apparently been deserted for years. Needing to stretch his legs, he pulled the car into the overgrown lane, shut off the engine, and got out. As he leaned against a fender, he studied the home. What paint that was left on the wooden slat siding was faded, a few of the windows were broken and now covered with boards, and the roof had been patched with flattened coffee cans. In a very real way, the house represented the hopelessness of his life.

As the speaker paused to allow the audience to grasp the verbal images he had painted, Stanphill must have seen the parallel between his own situation and that of the man behind the podium. His life had once seemed perfect, but now it appeared much more like that old house. It was empty and waiting to fall apart.

As the businessman picked up his story, Stanphill wondered how this old home figured into what was supposed to be a motivational speech centering on faith. After all, a vacant shack was not a beacon of light; it was more like a place of despair.

The speaker next explained that as he observed the lonely scene beyond the nose of his parked car, the front door opened and a small, barefoot girl, wearing a tattered dress and carrying a beat-up and broken doll, stepped onto the front stoop. The businessman was shocked. He couldn't believe that anyone could live in a place like this. The child waved before she began strolling through the overgrown yard. As she approached her guest, she smiled and asked, "Are you lost?"

"Kind of."

"Folks that drive down this road usually are lost," she noted.

It was then that the man made an observation. The little girl did not look sad or mournful but rather seemed to have no cares or worries. Finding himself headed toward poverty row had made him bitter. Why wasn't she? Unable to grasp how she so easily smiled, he posed a question.

"Why are you so happy?"

"I've got what I need," she replied. "And someday I'll have more than I need. You see that hill up there? One day, when things get better, my dad's going to build a big house on that spot."

The businessman glanced up to the top of the rise and then back to the child. As he scratched his head, he asked, "Do you really believe your father will build that house someday?"

"He's never lied to me. He says things will get better and then he will build it." As the visitor considered the child's innocent response, she added, "Believing makes you happy."

As the crowd listened intently to the speaker's story, Stanphill took a moment to consider the little girl's faith in her father. The businessman's voice pulled Stanphill's attention back to the podium.

Reaching into his pocket, the visitor gave the little girl a bit of money, hopped back into his car, and headed home. Returning to his plant, he gathered his remaining employees and told them that through God's grace they would all survive. He then vowed not to close his last business. And though it took years, the businessman rebuilt his empire.

As he ended his testimony, the crowd cheered and seemed inclined to lionize the man who had not given up. But as he made his way to his car, Stanphill thought only of the girl and her faith in her father. All the way home he considered how remarkable that parent must have been.

Inspired by what he had heard, when he got to his house, Stanphill sat down at the piano. Forgetting the heartache that was clouding his own life, he focused on the suffering that had ensnared so many on earth. The scars left first by the Depression and then by a war were everywhere. At that very moment in Europe, hundreds of thousands of refugees, including tens of thousands of orphaned children, had no homes. Many were sick and starving. In the United States, the hearts of widows and fatherless children might never mend. The only promise that any of those souls could cling to was that God had a place for them in heaven.

Pulling out a notebook, Stanphill quickly rewrote the story of the girl and her father into a hymn based on the words of Christ found in John 14. Within ten minutes, he had completed what would become his most popular composition.

During his time on earth, Jesus reminded his followers that to experience heaven, they had to become like little children. It therefore seems appropriate that the faith of a little girl inspired one of the most beloved gospel music songs in history. "Mansion over the Hilltop" is as simple as the child's words to the businessman, but it is a reminder to those fighting against the odds that there is the promise of an incredible life in heaven. The best way to see it is to embrace the faith of a child.

To learn more about Ira Stanphill, read his autobiography, *This Side of Heaven*, published by Hymntime Ministries in 1983.

Shall We Gather at the River

Then the angel showed me the river of life-giving water, shining like crystal, flowing from the throne of God and the Lamb through the middle of the city's main street. On each side of the river is the tree of life, which produces twelve crops of fruit, bearing its fruit each month. The tree's leaves are for the healing of the nations.

Revelation 22:1–2

Shall we gather at the river,
Where bright angel feet have trod,
With its crystal tide forever
Flowing by the throne of God?

Refrain:
Yes, we'll gather at the river,
The beautiful, the beautiful river;
Gather with the saints at the river
That flows by the throne of God.

On the margin of the river,
Washing up its silver spray,
We will talk and worship ever,
All the happy golden day.

Ere we reach the shining river,
Lay we every burden down;
Grace our spirits will deliver,
And provide a robe and crown.

At the smiling of the river,
Mirror of the Savior's face,
Saints, whom death will never sever,
Lift their songs of saving grace.

Soon we'll reach the silver river,
Soon our pilgrimage will cease;
Soon our happy hearts will quiver
With the melody of peace.

Water is a necessity of life. Beyond its uses for drinking and cleaning, water is used for swimming, fishing, and baptism. Seas, wells, and rivers serve as important biblical markers. Water is vital to the creation story and the narratives of Moses and Noah, the baptism of Christ, and Jesus walking on the water.

While controlled water is one of nature's greatest gifts, uncontrolled water is one of the world's most destructive forces. Floods and tidal waves change landscapes, destroy property, and have the power to take lives. Water can also effectively hide danger. In developing nations, a lack of access to safe water is the leading cause of death. So while water might soothe some hearts, it also frightens many. It took a man with a great knowledge of both the power of water and the fear created by water, along with an understanding of the Bible, to compose one of the best-known and most loved songs about heaven.

Robert Lowry was born in Philadelphia, Pennsylvania, on March 12, 1826. He grew up in an America that seemed to be constantly on the move. "Follow the river" became the cry of thousands of pioneers who longed for both adventure and the promise of a better life. There was a huge expanse of land begging to be developed, and people were following the Ohio River to the Mississippi and then, using other waterways, pushing into what had been wilderness.

During his youth, Lowry came to see rivers as routes to new lives and opportunities. As a child, Lowry observed families pack all their belongings, build a raft, and head west. While he eagerly read newspaper reports of the pioneers leading American expansion, he was focused on exploring a much different world. He wanted to lead people through the temptations of life and into an understanding and an appreciation of service to God. In other words, he felt the call to guide people to heaven.

While Lowry was growing up, only one-third of Americans attended church on a regular basis. Many American men of the mid-1800s were hard-living, risk takers who bragged about their sins. During that day, some viewed devout Christians as weak and baptism as a symbol of people with so little strength they had to admit their mistakes. As a high school student, the deeply religious Lowry decided to embrace the challenge of making hardened men take a second look at faith. To prepare himself to evangelize a nation in which two-thirds had no church affiliation, he studied theology at the University at Lewisburg (now Bucknell University). Beginning in 1854, he led a number of small New England congregations before being called to a position at the Hanson Place Baptist Church in Brooklyn.

After unpacking his bags, the young preacher found himself facing a congregation that was literally scared to death. The Civil War was raging, and many of the hardened men Lowry had vowed to lead to the Lord were now dying on battlefields. In the space of a few short months, life had become so cheap that funerals were more common than weddings. Soldiers, men who feared each day would be their last, spent their leaves drinking until they were numb. The homeless were everywhere. And hopeful waterways that once welcomed pioneers going west were now somber streams filled with military vessels and steamships transporting soldiers to battles. As Lowry preached, the faces in his pews reflected the mood of the country. A once optimistic nation was now hopeless and shaken. Many theologians were downcast and honestly believed the world was facing what some Christians called the end times.

On a hot July day, a weary Lowry left his church office and walked home. Alone, he read a few verses from the book of Revelation before lying down on a couch. He had hoped to rest, but sleep didn't come. Instead, he became immersed in the visions of John found in the Bible's final book. What he saw that day would inspire scores of sermons and one song.

Lowry's take on John's words in Revelation was different from that of a majority of scholars at the time. When using the final book in the Bible, most wrote commentaries or sermons that made people uncomfortable and insecure. Lowry's "Shall We Gather at the River" might have been inspired by writings concerning the destruction of the world, but the song was much more about life than death. While he fully realized the times seemed to have set a course leading straight to hell, he still recognized that individuals had a choice. A promise of heaven was waiting for all who accepted Christ. In the midst of all the bad news created by the war, this was great news! He just had to find a way to get people to hear it.

During Lowry's life, the most common place for family reunions was by streams or lakes. His new song might well have been inspired by this knowledge. After all, there is no greater reunion than what is waiting in heaven. His lyrics surely were also shaped by watching Americans fearfully look over rivers and wonder who was dying in battles on the other side. In time, rivers that separated the North from the South were often seen as the dividing point between life and death. Scores of preachers, books, and even motion pictures seized upon that imagery and used it to scare people. But Lowry chose to paint the river not as a place leading to death but as a route to be crossed in order to celebrate an eternal life. During the Civil War and the years after, this was exactly the message Americans needed to hear. Someday they would gather at the river and be reunited with those who had died in battle.

Late in his life, while teaching college at Lewisburg, Lowry described to a local reporter the day his best-known song was inspired.

> My imagination began to take itself wings. Visions of the future passed before me with startling vividness. The imagery of the apocalypse took the form of a tableau. Brightest of all were the throne, the heavenly river, and the gathering of the saints. . . . I began to wonder why the hymn writers had said so much about the river of death and so little about the pure water of life, clear as crystal, proceeding out of the throne of God and the Lamb. As I mused, the words began to construct themselves. They came first as a question of Christian inquiry, Shall we gather? Then they broke in chorus, Yes, we'll gather. On this question and answer the hymn developed itself. The music came with the hymn.[1]

Though "Shall We Gather at the River" was quickly published and placed in Baptist hymnals, its popularity was assured only when Dwight Moody used it night after night during his revival meetings. First in the United States and then in Europe, Moody employed Lowry's song as an invitation call. In 1880, on a trip to England to celebrate the one hundredth anniversary of the birth of the Sunday school movement, Lowry was shocked to discover just how well-known his hymn had become.

Lowry explained in Amos R. Wells's *A Treasure of Hymns*,

> I was in London and had gone to meeting in the Old Bailey to see some of the most famous Sunday school workers in the world. They were present from Europe, Asia, and America. I sat in a rear seat alone. After there had been a number of addresses delivered in various languages, I was preparing to leave, when the chairman of the meeting announced that the author of 'Shall We Gather at the River' was present, and I was requested by name to come forward. Men applauded and women waved their handkerchiefs as I went to the platform. It was a tribute to the hymn; but I felt, when it was over, that, after all, I had perhaps done some little good in the world, and I felt more than ever content to die when God called.[2]

The Jordan River is mentioned 190 times in the Bible and is a focal point in the Holy Land. Joshua knew the promised land was on the other side of the Jordan. It was also the place of Jesus's baptism. And since that day when John baptized Christ, tens of millions of people have waded into rivers as a pronouncement of their faith. Most believed that when they walked out of the water, they were beginning a new life. It is therefore only natural that crossing the Jordan has come to symbolize life after death. On the other side of the river is a place where love, grace, perfection, and peace reign. What Robert Lowry heard many hopeful people say still serves as a faith marker today: "Follow the river."

To learn more about Robert Lowry, read Amos R. Wells's *A Treasure of Hymns*, published by Fresh Fruits Press in 2015.

We'll Soon Be Done
with Troubles and Trials

> There's a season for everything
> and a time for every matter
> under the heavens.
>
> Ecclesiastes 3:1

Throughout his ministry, Jesus provided the formula for being the person God wants each of us to be. It began with being selfless. What Christ witnessed during his thirty-three years on earth, however, was that most people just couldn't give up what they had in order to help others. He also noticed that while forgiveness required living a truly selfless life, most of those he met found real forgiveness all but impossible. The fact was that, then and now, a majority of human beings think of their own wishes and needs long before they consider the needs of others.

With this in mind, it is hardly surprising that one of the most difficult things for anyone to comprehend is the joy found in doing things for others. Even when modern Christians consider the commitment of Mother Teresa, most can't begin to understand how someone who has given up everything they have to serve others can be anything but miserable and bitter. And the fact that this kind of thinking is so common means that few really grasp the way to become most like the person God intended them to be. Yet for those who observe dynamic spiritual living in action, it is obvious that happiness is strongest in the moments when people literally give up everything so that someone else may come closer to God.

In 1936, a twenty-six-year-old black preacher packed a suitcase and made a long train trip from rural Alabama to Dallas, Texas. Like others of his color, he rode in a segregated coach with few creature comforts. He couldn't even visit the train's dining car. This man's congregation, largely made up of maids and sharecroppers, worshiped in a drafty building, sat on worn-out, backless benches, and owned no songbooks. So they had to sing only what they had memorized. Their lack of hymnals reflected the state of their lives. They had nothing, and sadly, there seemed to be no hope for a better tomorrow. They would work until they died and likely never have more than a dollar or two in their pockets.

Though his parishioners paid him so little that he was forced to work odd jobs to feed his own family, Rev. Cleavant

Derricks never complained. Yes, he seemed destined to a life of poverty, and he accepted it as a part of his calling. In his mind, everything he had was on loan from God anyway. As the small, humble man, dressed in a suit and tie, entered the Dallas office of the Stamps-Baxter Music and Printing Company in the midst of the Great Depression, he smiled and offered a sincere apology. He explained that he was sorry for bothering the receptionist and didn't want to waste anyone's time, but he had written some songs he believed the publisher might be interested in. While filming the documentary *Say Amen Somebody*, Derricks would explain that some minutes later, a few disinterested employees sat around a piano in a practice room and watched thin fingers pound a keyboard. When Derricks began to sing, eyes lit up and heads shook. The audience was bored no more; they were obviously impressed.

Over the next few hours, Derricks explained that during a period when hard economic times had made poverty commonplace, his flock was the poorest of the poor. He further spelled out that his members were good people who loved the Lord, and so he had written these songs to offer a bit of hope. Sadly, it seemed that each member would have to wait until heaven to fully grasp the rewards of lives well lived. But, he added, his church was a wonderful place filled with God's grace and Spirit.

Those making the decisions at Stamps-Baxter informed Derricks that they wanted to gain the rights to two of his songs. When they asked what he wanted for "Just a Little

Talk with Jesus" and "We'll Soon Be Done with Troubles and Trials," the preacher suggested he be paid with an answered prayer. His flock had wanted songbooks for years. So why not trade the songs for some songbooks? Legal documents were quickly drawn up, and a smiling and thankful Derricks left with fifty new hymnals.

Derricks would never again travel to the publisher or check on his compositions. He was not even notified when his song about talking to Jesus in heaven was published. Still, thanks to quartets recording his pair of hymns, he was aware that others were getting to hear his work. And for the humble man of God, that, and the songbooks his congregation used during every worship service, was enough.

Forty years later, a small, elderly man with a big smile walked into the front door of a Nashville music publisher. It was a cold, windy morning, and only one of Canaanland's staff was in the office. As described in the liner notes of a record album called *Reverend Cleavant Derricks and Family Singing His Own Just a Little Talk with Jesus*, as Sylvia Mays looked up, the visitor tipped his hat and asked a simple question: "I have traveled from Washington, DC. Do you think anyone might be interested in hearing some gospel songs I've written?"

Mays had heard the pitch a thousand times, and usually what the guest thought was inspired music was anything but. Yet because it was such a bitterly cold day and the man had driven so far, she graciously asked if he had a tape. He retrieved a cassette and card from his pocket and handed them to Mays. She set them on her desk and asked, "Have you ever had anything published?"

He nodded. "As a matter of fact, I've even had a few recorded."

"Would I know any of them?"

The visitor smiled. "Have you ever heard of a song called 'Just a Little Talk with Jesus'? I wrote that and some others too."

Mays was shocked. She had been told the composer of that classic gospel song had disappeared years ago. Everyone assumed he had died. Finding her voice, she asked, "What's your name, sir?"

"I am Cleavant Derricks, but most people call me Rev."

At that moment, Mays was sure the only way this guest was Derricks was if she were talking to a ghost. But the guest was no ghost. After asking the man to take a seat, a perplexed Mays called her boss.

When J. Aaron Brown heard Mays's story, he was equally skeptical. He was sure the old man was an imposter. Nevertheless, he suggested Mays keep the visitor in the office until he could finish a recording session. Two hours later, the man who swore he was Cleavant Derricks was still patiently waiting when Brown walked in. After introductions were made, the producer escorted the visitor to his office. After the door was closed, the mysterious guest made a suggestion. "I wonder if you would let me sing for you?"

197

After just a few moments listening to the small man with a rich baritone sing a song about speaking to Jesus in heaven, Brown knew the mystery of what had happened to Cleavant Derricks had finally been solved. The guest had to be the legendary songwriter who had wandered into Stamps-Baxter forty years earlier and, after leaving with a box of hymnals, had never been heard from again.

Over the next few months, Brown and Derricks developed a deep friendship. What most impressed Brown was that Derricks held no bitterness about missing out on hundreds of thousands of dollars in royalties. Even decades later, he was still thrilled that his congregation had finally been able to sing from real hymnals. In fact, it seemed that everything about this man's life centered on what he could sacrifice to bring light to those living in darkness. With that in mind, Brown set to work righting a wrong.

"I was determined to get some of his royalty rights back," Brown explained upon release of the album that was made with Derricks, "so, I told his story to Frances Preston, the vice president of BMI. She convinced BMI to give him back royalties for the past six years and establish Derricks as the writer. He immediately received fourteen thousand dollars. He had never seen that much money at one time in his life."[1]

Brown did something else as well. He put Derricks in the studio to record both his new songs and his old ones. Using a 1930s blues rhythm, Derricks and his family cut "We'll Soon Be Done with Troubles and Trials." Though now in his seventies, the man brought the song to life in a way Brown could not have imagined. It was as if he was looking into heaven and watching Derricks sit down and talk to Jesus.

During more than fifty years of ministry, Derricks cared nothing about personal gain. He saw his calling as doing whatever was needed to guide lost souls to God and assure those at risk of losing all hope that there was a wonderful reward just out of sight. A few months after he recorded "Just a Little Talk with Jesus" for the first time, Cleavant Derricks died. After seventy-two years on earth, the preacher who had always given away far more than he had taken and guided so many to heaven finally got to sit down and talk to Jesus.

I Know Who Holds Tomorrow

I've commanded you to be brave and strong, haven't I? Don't be alarmed or terrified, because the LORD your God is with you wherever you go.

Joshua 1:9

On many occasions, Christ pointed out that people had become so focused on rituals and laws that they failed to see the needs of others around them. Christ taught that wealth had a way of becoming more important than serving God. At times, he even pointed out that worrying about things caused many to miss opportunities to do things that could make an impact. Those who listened to Christ surely understood where their focus needed to be but most likely just couldn't take their eyes off tomorrow long enough to see what needed to be done today.

Perhaps because his faith and convictions were so strong, Ira Stanphill always seemed to give up his tomorrows because of a commitment to serve today. Even when doing so meant sacrificing his dreams for the future, he would not turn his back on his word. And somehow, when he gave all his tomorrows to God, the future turned out to be more than he could have dreamed possible.

Stanphill's more than five hundred hymns can be seen as biographical. In direct and bluntly honest words, he revealed his faith as well as his doubts and fears. In reading his lyrics, people can see evidence of a man who stumbled from time to time but always had the strength to get back up. His songs also reveal a person who wrestled with choosing God's will over his own but in time came to realize that sticking with the Lord did more than pave his way to heaven; it brought a bit of heaven down to earth.

Born in 1914, Stanphill grew up in Kansas. At fifteen, he gave his life to the ministry, and at twenty-two, he began a career as a traveling evangelist. Over the next few decades, he shared the gospel in every corner of the United States and more than forty countries around the globe. Beyond his missionary work, he was a pioneer in his use of radio and television. But perhaps his most lasting contribution to the world was his music. Besides playing guitar, piano, accordion, saxophone, clarinet, and organ at the services he led, Stanphill had a gift for composing. And when he wrote songs, they almost always reflected his personal experiences.

In 1939, Stanphill married Zelma Lawson. Because Zelma was a gifted pianist and the daughter of a pastor, the marriage seemed to be ordained. Stanphill would tell friends and declare from the pulpit that his commitment to Zelma was one that would not be broken. Only death could force him to give up his vow to be hers and hers alone. When the couple had a son, everyone pointed to the Stanphills as models for a Christian family. They sang together, prayed together, and served God together. They were a team. Yet behind this image, cracks were beginning to appear that were threatening the union.

The growing demands for his preaching meant that Stanphill was often gone from home for long periods of time. Zelma, who had once accompanied her husband on his crusades, was now forced to stay behind to raise their child. Unable to cope with the pressure of spending so much time as a single parent, the new mother began to drink. As she grew even more isolated and alone, she also drifted into several affairs.

Over the course of the next five years, Stanphill did everything possible to provide the support his wife needed and to put their marriage back on track. Still, his efforts and prayers were for naught. Nine years after they were united in marriage, Zelma divorced the preacher and left with their child. The evangelist was devastated.

Stanphill found himself living in a world where friends and strangers alike bluntly pointed out that because of his

failed marriage, he was unfit to share God's Word. Wherever he traveled, he was confronted by church leaders who
suggested it would be best if he gave up his Christian work.
Many would have quit, but Stanphill was not one to cave
to pressure. He had done nothing wrong. Even in the face
of her affairs, he had never given up on Zelma or his marriage. Rather than publicly shame his ex-wife, he clung to
the biblical story of the woman caught in adultery and took
the high road. When given the opportunity to throw a stone,
he refused to do so.

His divorce might have closed many doors, but a new one
opened. Because of his experience, men and women who had
been through failed marriages sought him out for advice. He
was able to help them forgive themselves and move forward.
His words of comfort centered on not giving up on principles
and staying true to commitments. While the past couldn't be
changed and the future was unknown, there was still much joy
and satisfaction found in focusing on the present moment.

With fewer turning out to hear him at conventions and
revivals, Stanphill had little choice but to take a position with
the Bethel Temple in Dallas. The church served as home of
the Stamps School of Music. While he believed that being
surrounded by some of the greatest musicians in gospel
music would help him fine-tune his skills as a songwriter,
Stanphill's main reason for taking the position was his need
to rethink his ministry. He had to find a way for God to use
a man many Christians felt was not worthy of preaching.

At Bethel, Stanphill met Gloria Holloway. While the single woman's love of music served as the foundation for a deep friendship, her faith, seen in her actions and love, most impressed the preacher. The more he was around Gloria, the more the now very lonely man was attracted to her. As the months passed, he became convinced this was the person he should have married. She had all the qualities of the perfect partner. Still, rather than admit his feelings, he urged her to find someone else. When she demanded to know why, he explained that many churches and Christian organizations would not accept a man who had been divorced and then remarried. So if he married the woman he loved, he would be forced to give up his calling. He simply could not do that. He further broke Gloria's heart by adding that he had made a vow to be true to his wife until death. Just because she had broken her pledge did not mean he could break his. That vow, he said, would keep him from ever marrying again.

As he pushed the woman he loved out of his life, Stanphill plunged into the darkness of depression. He began to see his call to the ministry as setting in motion the events that led to his divorce. And now that same ministry was keeping him from a marriage he envisioned being filled with joy and love. In other words, his happiness and his future had been stolen from him. So as he sat alone, he couldn't help but whisper, "Why?"

Like a man who had been given only six months to live, Stanphill felt like giving up. He honestly figured his future was hopeless and he would forever be alone. His only consolation was knowing he had a place in heaven. As he bowed his head and prayed, he thought he heard a voice asking, "Why are you so worried about tomorrow?"

As he considered that question, Stanphill couldn't help but remember all the times he had urged people to live in the moment. He had begged them to do what they could right now because the future was in God's hands. With that thought burning in his mind, Stanphill rushed to a piano and quickly wrote a song. When he finished "I Know Who Holds Tomorrow," he was no longer asking, "Why me?"

When scores of well-known entertainers recorded "I Know Who Holds Tomorrow" and letters began pouring in saying that it contained a message thousands needed to hear to get through difficult times in their lives, Stanphill saw his faith renewed. With passion and zeal, he embraced his promise to serve God today and leave tomorrow to Jesus.

Months later, Stanphill was working on a new song when his phone rang. A somber voice informed him that his ex-wife had been tragically killed in an automobile accident. The next few days were a blur. Yet he felt no bitterness as he bid farewell to the woman who had cost him so much. In fact, he had prayed for Zelma's well-being and happiness every day since their divorce. He was deeply sorry she had never experienced a life rich in happiness and joy. After a final goodbye and with his son once again by his side, Stanphill returned to Dallas.

Over the next year, the father and the boy built a new life, and then something completely unplanned and unexpected happened: Gloria Holloway and Ira Stanphill accidently crossed paths. A few months later, they were married.

For many Christians, faith and worry are opposing forces constantly fighting for control. Even on the best of days, some can't help but feel apprehensive about tomorrow. Many become so consumed with their concerns about the future that they fail to use their lives in the way the Lord intended in the present. In a very real sense, they are worrying their lives away. While heaven is a promise we can look forward to, Christ taught us to leave the future to God and enjoy the blessings and potential of each moment. Like a person given six months to live, we should use, embrace, and revel in this day as if there is no tomorrow.

When the Roll
Is Called Up Yonder

The scripture says, All who have faith in him won't be put to shame. There is no distinction between Jew and Greek, because the same Lord is Lord of all, who gives richly to all who call on him. All who call on the Lord's name will be saved.

Romans 10:11–13

When the trumpet of the Lord shall sound,
and time shall be no more,
and the morning breaks, eternal, bright and fair;
when the saved of earth shall gather
over on the other shore,
and the roll is called up yonder, I'll be there.

Refrain:
When the roll is called up yonder,
when the roll is called up yonder,

when the roll is called up yonder,
when the roll is called up yonder, I'll be there.

On that bright and cloudless morning
when the dead in Christ shall rise,
and the glory of his resurrection share;
when his chosen ones shall gather
to their home beyond the skies,
and the roll is called up yonder, I'll be there.

Let us labor for the Master
from the dawn till setting sun,
let us talk of all his wondrous love and care;
then when all of life is over,
and our work on earth is done,
and the roll is called up yonder, I'll be there.

Each of us grows up in a world where, in one form or another, attendance is taken. For many, this practice begins in school. Almost every church marks members present or absent. In the military, there is roll call. Civic and social clubs almost always note who is at their meetings. Congress keeps tabs on elected officials. And in the workplace, checking in, sometimes by punching a time card, is usually required. Since the beginning, people have kept tabs on people. In fact, in our modern world, there is an app for that.

In 1894, James M. Black was a Christian layman and music teacher. He had been born in New York in 1856 and as a child had moved to Williamsport, Pennsylvania. From his youth, he was active in the local Methodist Episcopal Church. About the time of his thirtieth birthday, he volunteered to be the Sunday school director and set to work to enlarge the scope and reach of that program.

Children's ministries were areas in which Black felt growth was of greatest importance. With that in mind, he visited schools, youth clubs, and sporting events in an effort to meet children and offer invitations to join the church each Sunday morning for a lesson and a snack. He also emphasized to kids already in his church their need to bring friends to class each week. One day while shopping, he noted a girl wandering down the street. Her clothes were shabby and torn, her arm scraped, her face dirty, and her hair uncombed. Her shyness was obvious as she kept her eyes down when approaching strangers. At that moment, Black was not looking for another body to fill a chair at the church but was concerned about this child's well-being. Calmly, he moved down the street to where she was peering into a shop window. As he stood beside her, he introduced himself and started a conversation. He found out her name and that she was fourteen and even obtained information about the area where she lived. Based on her appearance, he was hardly surprised it was on the wrong side of the tracks.

The next day he used his contacts with school officials to uncover more of her story. The girl's father was unemployed. He was surly, vulgar, and abusive. He was also a drunk. Through his language and actions, he had brought great shame to his family. Even worse, his lust for alcohol meant his daughter often missed meals. If ever someone was what Jesus called "the least of these," it was this child.

When Black ran into the girl again, he invited her to attend Sunday school. He promised that she would receive a lesson and a chance for a meal. Once she began Sunday school, she never missed. Soon she was also there on Sunday nights and Wednesdays. In time, she even joined the youth group.

One of the traditions of Black's youth group was responding to the roll call by citing a favorite Scripture passage. The child from the poor side of town always had a Bible verse ready. So it came as a shock when, on a cold winter's night, Black announced her name and she didn't answer. Because of her loyalty, Black was concerned. In fact, he was so troubled that he opted to change his lesson to one that centered on the Book of Life. This Book is mentioned many places within the Scriptures, and Black also cited passages in Revelation.

Many churches, including Black's, had their own Book of Life. It contained all the names of members both past and present. It also noted those who had made significant gifts to the church or had died and gone on to heaven. Therefore, the children in the youth group were anxious to find their names in the pages.

After the meeting concluded and the teenagers left, Black almost went home, but as he was locking the church door, he stopped short. The girl's absence deeply bothered him. Church had become her refuge. She loved being inside its walls. She was there even when she had to walk through rain or snow. Something had to be wrong. In an impulsive move, he decided to go to the wrong side of the tracks to find out what had happened.

Black was apprehensive as he knocked on the door. If the father was drunk, things could get ugly. But instead of a parent, a doctor answered. He explained that the girl, likely due to her frail nutritional state, had caught pneumonia. After stepping into what was more a tiny shack than a house, Black visited the child and offered a prayer. How he wished he could have done more.

Black left that night feeling confident the child would survive. But each day when he returned, she seemed to grow weaker. Finally, two weeks later, she lapsed into a coma and never regained consciousness. As he confronted her death, the Sunday school teacher questioned if he could have done more for the abused child. Perhaps he could have gotten authorities to move her to a children's home. Perhaps if he had acted, she wouldn't be dead.

That night he shared his grief with his wife. He felt that if the girl had been born in other circumstances, things would have been very different. Black's wife, in an effort to comfort him, mentioned that the child was in a much better home now. The woman then added that the girl was now with a Father who deeply loved her.

With those words still lingering in the air, Black moved to a piano and began to play. As his fingers touched the keys, he was reminded of a story he had heard as a boy. During the Civil War, a badly injured soldier was brought straight from a battlefield to a hospital. It was apparent there was nothing the doctors could do for him. So they cleaned him up, moved him to a bed, and asked a nurse to give him whatever he wanted. As his breathing grew more labored, the young man lapsed into unconsciousness. About an hour later, with no warning, he sat up in his bed and yelled, "Here!" The nurse rushed across the room and asked if he needed anything. He assured her he didn't. Then she inquired as to why he had spoken. He whispered his explanation. "They were calling the roll in heaven, and I was answering to my name."

Was the story true? Black didn't know, but the story coupled with the child's death served as immediate inspiration. Within seconds, a tune popped into his head. Words followed next. Within just a few minutes, he had finished "When the Roll Is Called Up Yonder." The next day he taught it to the church choir. The first time it was sung in public was at the child's funeral. It not only brought peace to the children of the youth group but also focused Black's mind on the image of the girl calling out her name in heaven.

In 2003, family friends of mine decided to attend a high school basketball game. The mother and father and their six children loaded up in a decade-old van and drove to the gym. The contest between the two rivals was close and in doubt until the final minute. Therefore, as the family made their way out of the gym, they were revved up and excited. The hour was late, and it was a weeknight, so when they got home, the mother ordered her children to get cleaned up and ready for bed. Only when she walked into each of their rooms, as was her habit, did she realize that their nine-year-old daughter was missing. Without noticing, they had left her at the school.

Immediately, the father jumped back into the van. After parking in front of the gym, he raced through the front doors. As he entered, he noted a few team members and parents talking on the court and a janitor cleaning up the stands. And on a bench, smiling, sat his daughter. She didn't seem to have a concern in the world. When her father asked if she had been worried, she shrugged and announced, "I knew you'd come back for me as soon as Mom did the bedtime roll call."

It is written that God knows every hair on our heads and even sees the sparrow when it falls. The Lord is always there for us on earth and will be waiting for us in heaven. And when he calls our names from the Book of Life, we will shout them out with joy.

When the Morning Comes

Stop collecting treasures for your own benefit on earth, where moth and rust eat them and where thieves break in and steal them. Instead, collect treasures for yourselves in heaven, where moth and rust don't eat them and where thieves don't break in and steal them.

Matthew 6:19–20

Trials dark on ev'ry hand, and we cannot understand
All the way that God will lead us to that blessed
 promised land;
But He'll guide us with His eye, and we'll follow till
 we die,
We will understand it better by and by.

Refrain:
By and by, when the morning comes,
All the saints of God are gathering home.
We will tell the story how we've overcome
We will understand it better by and by.

We are often destitute of the things that life demands,
Want of shelter and of food, thirsty hill and barren
    land;
But we're trusting in the Lord, and according to
    His word,
We will understand it better by and by.

Temptations, hidden snares, often take us unawares,
And our hearts are made to bleed, for each
    thoughtless word or deed;
And we wonder why the test, when we try to do our
    best,
But we'll understand it better by and by.

*D*uring his ministry, Jesus was often ridiculed for spending time with the wrong people. In the Bible, we read about Christ choosing to be with the marginalized rather than the ruling class. The very ones others ignored felt his touch and love. Through words, actions, and attention, he gave them a sense of value. In Jesus's eyes, they were equal to even a king. Imagine what this affirmation meant to a leper, the woman caught in adultery, the woman at the well, or even the tax collector. But it is also wise to visualize how this looked to the establishment of that time. Even many respected religious people wondered what Jesus was doing hanging out with *those* people.

To this day, there is a sense of hopelessness in being seen as a second-class human being. Being labeled as such affects every facet of a person's life. There are things some are barred from doing, places some can't enter, jobs some can't apply for. There is also that ever-present sense of disdain when people approach. In a very real sense, the marginalized constantly question their value and worth. No one likely knew the weight of this struggle better than Charles Tindley.

Tindley was born in Maryland in 1851. His father was a slave who was sold to another plantation owner when Tindley was just a toddler. His mother, a free black woman who worked as a servant, died before the boy learned to talk. Though technically free by law, he was given to slaves to raise. They became his family, and he stayed with them until the Civil War ended. When Lee surrendered to Grant, Tindley, then fourteen, was told he was free—but that meant nothing. To make a living, he did a slave's work, spending fourteen hours a day in the fields employed by the same people who had once owned his father. And even though he could legally claim he had been free since birth, because of his black skin, he was viewed in the same way as any former slave.

Tindley lived in a world where he was told to stay in his place. He worked a job for which he was paid far less than a white man doing the same labor. He was literally a second-class citizen with few rights. He was neither valued nor respected. The horses on the plantation were treated better than he was. No one had to explain that the world was unfair; he witnessed that fact each day.

In the evening, when almost everyone else rested, the teenager was so driven to grow beyond expectations that he ran ten miles to attend a night school. On Sundays, he went to a small church with former slaves. There was one Bible in the building, and because Tindley was the only one who had been given schooling, he was always asked to read it. In time, reading the Bible aloud each Sunday morning would change the direction of his life.

Tindley grew into a huge man, more than six feet four inches tall. His shoulders were the width of an axe handle. With his dark eyes, huge hands, booming voice, and ebony skin, he cut an imposing figure. In time, he came to realize that physical presence paled when compared to knowledge. Thus, in every spare moment, he read everything he could lay his hands on. His thirst for knowledge drove him as a teen and pushed him the remainder of his life.

In his early twenties, he married a woman he had met in church, left the only home he had ever known, and searched for a place where he would be treated as an equal. While he failed to find a place where a black man was seen in the same way as a white man, he did discover a large African American community in Philadelphia. After negotiating the right to use their library, Tindley took a position as the janitor of the John Wesley Methodist Episcopal Church. He had been there only a few weeks when he received a call to preach, but at that point, he didn't feel fully equipped to step behind a pulpit and deliver a message. To prepare himself to explain the Scriptures, he devoted several years to studying Hebrew, Greek, business, and theology. Only after believing he had the education needed to teach others did he accept a pastorate.

Several years and five churches later, Tindley, now in his late forties, returned to the John Wesley Methodist Episcopal Church. Under his leadership, the congregation grew from 130 to more than a thousand in a year. His preaching style was so dynamic and powerful that even whites began to attend the church to see what all the fuss was about.

By this time, Tindley had become a master Bible scholar. He had read hundreds of books that looked at faith from every direction. He had also developed an incredible skill of putting things into a perspective a child could grasp while also delivering words that challenged adults. And as a way of emphasizing certain points, he wrote songs and wove them into his sermons. He employed his rich baritone voice when delivering these musical messages.

Behind the scenes, Tindley was also doing all he could to push for equal rights. He met with the mayor, formed associations to encourage businesses to hire blacks, set up food kitchens for people of all colors, and provided night school education for the illiterate. Inevitably, change came slowly, and the songs he composed for his sermons, such as "I Shall Overcome" and "Stand by Me," presented the need for patience. But these hymns were not written as a white flag of defeat; they were a call to keep moving, growing, and working, because Jesus was on the side of those the world saw as having little or no value.

In his messages, Tindley constantly pointed out that he had lived the life of a slave. He had faced a world where his race had few opportunities for growth, expression, and advancement. He knew there were few jobs that offered any hope of progress, and many schools, theaters, stores, and cafés were closed to those of color. And though he knew this wasn't right, he didn't know when things would change. That question of change, the one thing everyone in his congregation prayed to see, was the one that haunted his every waking hour.

One Sunday morning in 1904, Tindley stood in front of his congregation and sang "When the Morning Comes." His latest composition reflected something he deeply believed and could clearly be seen in Christ's ministry: the Lord has no favorites. And those who never give up on faith will be rewarded with an equal place in heaven.

While Tindley's new hymn was well received, it didn't offer a magic fix. Most African Americans in his congregation wanted their struggles justified at *this* moment, not in the future. They wanted their pastor to give them something tangible they could hang on to now. Instead, the preacher reminded his people that the disciples also wanted immediate answers. They too wanted to level the ground and have power placed in their hands. They too grew tired of the trials. But in spite of their tribulations, eleven of the twelve never gave up, and by and by they were reunited with Jesus.

"When the Morning Comes" was quickly published and made its way to black churches across the country. Then in 1920 something remarkable happened. The Southern Baptists, at that time a segregated union of churches, put the black preacher's composition into their official hymnal. In a very real sense, this marked a monumental breaking of the color line and must have pleased the son of a slave as much as any award he ever received.

Tindley's most famous sermon involved a peach tree. In that message, he painted a picture of a tree so heavy with fruit that the limbs bowed and reached down to the ground. Using this illustration, he explained that from this tree even a small child could pick a peach. He then suggested that it was a Christian's calling to bend low and lift others up. That simple act would provide each person with value and assure them they were equal. He concluded by noting that the peach tree represented Christ and if they wanted to follow Jesus, they would give and forgive as freely as he had.

By the end of the twenties, Tindley's congregation had grown to more than ten thousand members. About a third of those who attended each Sunday morning were white. He was so well respected that Ivy League seminaries sent their students to his church to learn from the man they called "the prince of preaching." Yet in truth, when he died in 1933, he was still seen as a second-class citizen.

A study of the life of Christ clearly shows his love for every man and woman no matter their station or race. So even though the color of his skin barred Tindley from many places on earth, when he drew his last breath and the next morning came, he was treated as an equal in heaven. Thus, his earthly message was fulfilled and his prayers were answered.

To learn more about Charles Tindley, read Ralph H. Jones's *The Prince of Preachers*, published by Abingdon Press in 1982.

I Wouldn't Take Nothing
for My Journey Now

❖ ——— ❖ ——— ❖ ——— ❖

He was in the wilderness for forty days, tempted by Satan.
He was among the wild animals, and the angels took care
of him.

Mark 1:13

*R*ight after his baptism by John the Baptist, Jesus
spent forty days fasting in the wilderness. The toll
of that kind of deprivation is beyond comprehension. Only
a few, such as those who have survived concentration camps
or been POWs, can begin to grasp the experience. It was
while fasting, when Jesus was at his physical bottom, that
he faced one of his greatest challenges—one that mirrored
a challenge every person will encounter at some time. The
response to such a challenge defines our character and our
ultimate destination.

While Jesus might have begun his spiritual quest alone, he was soon joined by an uninvited and unwelcomed guest. Why did Satan, history's greatest salesman, choose to confront God's Son at this time? There are many theories, but perhaps the soundest reasoning centers on the fact that while Jesus was fully God, he was also fully human. Thus, he had the same basic needs of every person who had ever lived. And while fasting, he was weak.

It seems natural that Satan first seized upon Jesus's hunger. Christ was suffering. His human body was demanding fuel. So because Jesus had the power of God, Satan suggested that Jesus turn stones into bread. When Jesus said no, the devil did not quit. Just like with all other humans, Satan's con was just starting. It was his nature to offer a number of temptations as a way of altering a life and creating a detour off the heavenly highway onto the road to hell.

For Jesus, Satan's next stop involved a trip to Jerusalem. As the two stood on top of the temple, the devil suggested that Christ prove his power by leaping to the ground below. Satan intimated that surely God would reach down and save Jesus from death or injury. This would prove his power to the world. Once again, Jesus turned down the opportunity.

Finally, a disappointed Satan took Jesus to a point where they could see the entire earth. As they looked down, the devil suggested that if Jesus were to turn his back on God, then all of this could be his. With that one act of betrayal, Christ the man could become the most powerful person on the planet. Riches, fame, and influence awaited him. Unmoved, Jesus ordered Satan to hit the trail.

Once alone, Jesus was visited by visitors from heaven. Rather than tempt Jesus, these angels, along with the wild animals in the desert, ministered to his needs. In a very real sense, he was rewarded for continuing on the journey his Father had laid out for him.

In many ways, the accounts of the temptation of Christ found in Mark, Luke, and John are some of the most dynamic verses in the Bible. Refusing Satan's offers is a key element of the early part of Christ's life. The accounts also reveal that Jesus the man faced the same choices we do in relation to turning from a moral path. The stories of the temptation of Christ prove that he can relate to what we feel and experience, and through the scriptural accounts of Satan confronting Jesus, we can see the proper way to handle temptation.

As a teenager, Rusty Goodman was a featured part of his brother's gospel music group—and a young man who walked the straight and narrow. When Howard Goodman and his wife, Vestal, moved to Kentucky to preach, Rusty, then almost twenty, entered the military. Upon mustering out, Rusty joined country music groups in Louisiana and tried his hand at songwriting. When Elvis and rock 'n' roll became hot, the fledgling tunesmith jumped in with both feet. He was bound and determined to get rich writing songs for rock 'n' roll royalty. After a series of rejections and some bad lifestyle choices, the young husband and father wound up broke and disillusioned.

As he made his long trip to the bottom, Rusty gave in to a wide variety of temptations. During this period, the night life constantly called, while the mornings served to remind him of the high price of his actions. Unable to find success or peace, and afraid he would wind up dying like one of his idols, Hank Williams, a lonely alcoholic, Rusty strolled into a small church in Baton Rouge. Feeling as if he had finally come home, he walked the aisle and confessed his sins. After the service, he gathered up his family, rented a trailer, hitched it to his car, packed all the family's belongings, and drove to Kentucky to see Howard.

On an early Saturday morning, Rusty opened his brother's front door and proudly announced that he had bottomed out. All he owned was in the trailer, and he, his wife, and his daughter were essentially homeless. He had no job or money, but he claimed it was the happiest day of his life because he had turned his back on temptation and was once more walking with the Lord. Mirroring a biblical parable, Howard opened the door to the wandering brother.

As he looked for work, Rusty began to play the organ at Howard's church. After services, he stayed in the building and once again tried his hand at songwriting. This time he wasn't attempting to write the next hit for Elvis but rather was voicing the thankfulness found in his heart. Within a few weeks, one of those songs of testimony, "The Answer Is on the Way," was sold to a publisher. A few months later, as more of his compositions were published, Rusty and Howard decided it was time to bring the family back together. Yet it would take a man few noticed to pave the way for the Happy Goodmans to become one of the most important forces in gospel music.

In the rural Kentucky town that served as the Goodmans' base of operations lived Shorty Carter. There can be no doubt that he was one of the most unusual individuals ever to come out of the backwoods. He could be both funny and aggravating. Sadly, the diminutive man was developmentally disabled. Though already into middle age, in many ways he was like a child.

Life had not been fair to Shorty. He had no money and a shack for a home, wore clothes given to him by others, and was the butt of jokes and pranks. Both children and adults constantly picked on him. Still, even the cruelest words could not break the man's spirit. He never quit smiling and always greeted others with a happy "Hello."

While he belonged to no specific congregation, Shorty never missed an opportunity to worship. Sometimes he attended three or four churches in one day. Whether it was a Methodist, Assembly of God, Baptist, or Presbyterian church, people groaned when Shorty entered because they knew at some point during the service he would ask to speak. After a while, most preachers learned to ignore Shorty's request. In fact, some even suggested the man would be better served if he didn't go to church at all . . . at least not their church.

One day during a service in which the Goodman family was singing, Shorty raised his hand. Amazing everyone, Howard allowed the small man to talk. Over the course of several minutes, Shorty spoke of how hard his life was and how people didn't understand him. He also talked about being poor and mistreated. Then he turned to how much God loved and accepted him and what a joy it was to know that God had a purpose for his life. And because of that love and acceptance, the devil wasn't going to tempt him to get even with those who spoke harshly and made his life miserable with their jabs and pranks. Before sitting down, Shorty smiled, looked up at the Happy Goodmans, and declared, "You know, I wouldn't take nuthin' for my journey now."

Though not eloquent, Shorty's words were both haunting and deeply spiritual. Unlike so many who were bitter because life seemed unfair, Shorty accepted it as part of a fallen and imperfect world. In the midst of misery, he found joy.

Not long after being allowed to speak, Shorty Carter grew sick. As he lay on his deathbed, Rusty Goodman went to see him. The little man who had never been given a break looked up at his guest and whispered, "I wouldn't take nuthin' for my journey now."

Inspired by the words of a dying man most in town viewed as a misfit, Rusty returned home and composed one of the most uplifting gospel standards of the 1960s. In its lyrics and upbeat melody, "I Wouldn't Take Nothing for My Journey Now" was a song reflecting both Shorty Carter's view of life and the experience of Christ being tempted by Satan. The lyrics clearly painted that while life might be a trial, thanks to Jesus, there is a reward waiting. That reward trumps every temptation the devil can offer.

"I Wouldn't Take Nothing for My Journey Now" put the Happy Goodmans on the map. It sold millions of records, won countless awards, and would be recorded by some of the biggest names in religious music. More importantly, it presented a road map on how to make it through hardships on earth by always keeping an eye fixed on heaven.

In 1990, Rusty Goodman was struck by cancer. He was just fifty-seven and at the peak of his career. But just like the little man who had once inspired "I Wouldn't Take Nothing for My Journey Now," Rusty didn't give up, grow bitter, or ask, "Why me?" Even at the end, when pain was ripping his body apart, the songwriter told guests, "I wouldn't take nothing for my journey now." And at that moment, with Rusty so close to heaven, the devil, just as he had done when he had failed to tempt Christ, walked away defeated.

To learn more about the Happy Goodmans, read Vestal Goodman and Ken Abraham's *Vestal!: "Lord, I Wouldn't Take Nothin' for My Journey Now,"* published by Water-Brook Press in 1999.

Victory in Jesus

I've said these things to you so that you will have peace in me. In the world you have distress. But be encouraged! I have conquered the world.

John 16:33

Webster defines victory as "the overcoming of an enemy or antagonist." Another definition is "achievement of mastery of success in a struggle or endeavor against odds or difficulties."[1] From an early age, most people are tossed into activities in which the purpose is to win. It might be a sporting event, a playground game, or even an academic contest. Even at church, children are encouraged to win "sword drills" and Bible memorization games. There are often prizes for those who finish first. It seems that from the cradle we teach children that if they don't win, they must be a loser.

The games might shift to a different venue and be played with more complex rules, but most adults are involved in vocations that are competitive by nature, and results are usually measured to determine a winner. Who sold the most product in a week or whose team assembled the most items often means the difference between holding on to a job and being fired. Thus, there is a constant fight to be seen as the victor.

For centuries, life has been called a game. Many have also called living "a series of struggles to survive to the next day." In the end, however, not even wealth and position can produce a winner in the game of life. At least not by society's definition. For every person born, the end results are the same. One of the greatest hymns suggests that the scoring method most used is deeply flawed.

Eugene Bartlett's compositions have touched hundreds of millions. His works most often reflect the Missouri native's optimistic viewpoint and wonderful sense of humor. And he had every right to be upbeat. Even during the Great Depression, he prospered. While many of his neighbors lost homes and farms and were forced to hit the road to find work, he seemed to be on top of the world. Even when thousands of financial institutions went under, his Siloam Springs, Arkansas, publishing company sold hundreds of thousands of pieces of music. So with money in the bank, he could have sat back and lived the high life, but Bartlett was bent on sharing his faith with others. In his chosen role as a witness for God, he was constantly on the move. Even in his early fifties, he kept a travel schedule that would have worn out most people half his age. Why? Because he was a person who felt a need to define victory in a new way.

In 1939, Bartlett was returning from another long tour. Just minutes before his train pulled into the station near his Ozark Mountains home, he began to feel ill. A headache quickly became something more. As a major stroke raced through his nervous system, Bartlett was brought to his knees in pain. When carried from the train, he could not speak. A doctor was called, and the tests that followed proved the composer's life was essentially over. While in time he might gain back a few of his skills, he would surely never again be the man known for his boundless energy and wit. Even the most optimistic view forecasted that Bartlett would spend whatever time he had left confined to his room. Worst of all, the person who had performed before royalty and presidents would likely never again sing a note.

Those who knew him well watched Bartlett closely. Until the stroke, everything he had attempted had been easily realized. But now, with the once great man so humbled by his body's failure, surely he would lose his faith and demand to know why God had stilled his voice. So the doubters sat back and waited for him to cry out, "Why me?"

Over the next few months, as he wasted away in bed, Bartlett showed no bitterness. His smile might have looked a bit different than it had when all his muscles were working, but crooked or not, it was still there whenever anyone came to see him. Though speaking was sometimes difficult and his voice slurred, during his conversations he refused to focus on his limitations. Remarkably, even though his life had shrunk from circling the globe and performing before thousands to living in just a small part of his house and meeting one person at a time, he kept reminding others of all the blessings he could claim.

During this time, the most difficult thing for his family to watch was Bartlett trying to write. Before the stroke, he could pen a hymn in minutes. Now it took him that long to push his pencil into his hand and scribble a single word. Just writing two lines completely wore him out. Worst of all, his thoughts had to be pulled from a mind that seemed to have one objective: turning every function of his body off. And still Bartlett kept slowly plugging along. After months of painful work, he dropped the pencil and pushed the paper toward his wife. In a halting, weak voice, he told her he believed he had successfully written his musical testimony. He thought it was framed in such a way that others would understand that there was a victorious moment in death that made every triumph in life seem trivial.

"Victory in Jesus" represented a different type of song for Bartlett. It was deeply personal. In the lyrics, he revealed his weakness and pain as much as his strength and faith. Yet much like "Everybody Will Be Happy Over There," "Camping on Canaanland," and "Set My Soul Afire," his last song embraced the optimism that defined his life. The price Jesus had paid on the cross made each Christian a winner. Most importantly, the very moment when everything seemed lost was the moment everything was gained.

On January 25, 1941, Eugene Bartlett died. He was just fifty-five years old. The last song he wrote, the final note of a remarkable career, is now the one that defines not only his gifts to Christian music but also the man himself. In the face of a stroke that left him only a shell of what he once had been, when his horizon had been whittled down from a wide world of travel to just a few small rooms, facing a future with far more limits than opportunities, Bartlett had somehow seen a victory most people missed. And more than eight decades later, his final curtain call is still bringing people hope.

A dear friend of mine battled cancer three times in ten years. While the disease robbed her of everything from her job to her ability to bear children, it couldn't touch her spirit. On a day-by-day basis, she found things that made her laugh and brought her joy. And with no thoughts of her limitations, she looked for ways she could lift others up.

When the cancer came back the third time, I asked Nancy if she ever demanded to know, "Why me?" Her answer left me stunned.

"No, I say why not me. I'd rather have cancer than see my loved ones battle it. Cancer gives me a perspective of the value of each day. It also allows me the chance to help others who find themselves in the same fight that I'm in."

During her final days, she clung to "Victory in Jesus" like a lifeboat.

Another person who left the world far too soon was Roger Bennett. The pianist, singer, composer, and keyboardist for the famed Cathedral Quartet battled leukemia for the final twelve years of his life. Bennett mirrored Bartlett when in the midst of dealing with a disease he knew would snuff out his life, he wrote a song based on what he had discovered in the Bible: "I've Read the Back of the Book and We Win."

For a Christian, life might be a struggle, but it is not a losing game. In fact, the big victory happens when the final breath is taken. That is when faith is fully affirmed. With that win assured, there is no reason to worry or fret. Each day should therefore be joyous and full. That is the profound message found in "Victory in Jesus" as well as the message of the Savior who inspired the song. We have already won, and it's time to act like winners!

Acknowledgments

Thanks to Jamie Chavez for her hard work in editing and wonderful insights that made this work possible.

Notes

Face to Face

1. Charles Hutchinson Gabriel, *The Singers and Their Songs* (London: Forgotten Books, 2017).

Glory Train

1. Baker Knight, interview by Ace Collins, January 1998.

Peace in the Valley

1. Michael P. Graves and David Fillingim, *More Than "Precious Memories"* (Macon, GA: Mercer University Press, 2004).

This World Is Not My Home

1. Scott Cuffe, *Bat Masterson's Last Words* (Lulu.com, 2015).

The Unclouded Day

1. Josiah Alwood, "A Rainbow at Midnight and a Song in the Morning," *Christian Conservator*, February 26, 1896.

Walk Dem Golden Stairs

1. Quotes in this chapter taken from Gordon Stoker, interview by Ace Collins, January 1999.

Shall We Gather at the River

1. Amos R. Wells, *A Treasure of Hymns* (Wilmore, KY: First Fruits Press, 2015).

2. Wells, *A Treasure of Hymns*.

We'll Soon Be Done with Troubles and Trials

1. J. Aaron Brown, interview by Ace Collins, February 1976.

Victory in Jesus

1. *Merriam-Webster*, s.v. "victory," accessed May 8, 2019, http://unab ridged.merriam-webster.com/collegiate/victory.

Citing his Arkansas heritage, Christy Award winner **Ace Collins** defines himself as a storyteller. In that capacity, Collins has authored more than eighty books that have sold more than 2.5 million copies for twenty-five publishers. His catalogue includes novels, biographies, and children's works as well as books on history, culture, and faith. Beyond books, Collins has penned more than two thousand magazine features.

He has been the featured speaker at the National Archives Distinguished Lecture Series, hosted a television special, and appeared on every network's morning television show. He has also appeared on news and entertainment programming on CNN, MSNBC, and CNBC and does scores of radio interviews each year. His speaking engagements have taken him from churches and corporations to the America's Dog Museum in St. Louis and the National Archives in Washington, DC. Collins has penned several production shows and regularly speaks to college classes on the art of writing.

Ace's hobbies include sports, restoring classic cars, Wurlitzer jukeboxes, and playing guitar. He is married to Dr. Kathy Collins, chair of the Department of Education at Ouachita Baptist University. The couple lives in Arkadelphia, Arkansas, and has two grown sons.

Connect with
ACE

To learn more about Ace's writing, visit

AceCollins.com

 AceCollins   AuthorAceCollins